# THE TAIL

# THE TAIL

## HOW ENGLAND'S SCHOOLS FAIL ONE CHILD IN FIVE – AND WHAT CAN BE DONE

Edited by Paul Marshall

*Contributions by*
Chris Amadeo, Dale Bassett, Sophy Blakeway, Kevan Collins,
Frank Field, Chris Husbands, Tina Isaacs, Michael Keating,
Danny Kruger, Tim Leunig, Stephen Machin, Paul Marshall,
Chris Paterson, Olmo Silva, Charlie Taylor, James Toop,
Tim Weedon, Patrick White and Gill Wyness

**P**
PROFILE BOOKS

First published in Great Britain in 2013 by
PROFILE BOOKS LTD
3A Exmouth House
Pine Street
London EC1R 0JH
www.profilebooks.com

1 3 5 7 9 10 8 6 4 2

A CIP catalogue record for this book is available from the British Library.

Typeset in Times by MacGuru Ltd
info@macguru.org.uk
Printed and bound in Britain by
Clays, Bungay, Suffolk

ISBN 978 1 78125 167 6
eISBN: 978 1 84765 988 0

The paper this book is printed on is certified by the © 1996 Forest Stewardship
Council A.C. (FSC). It is ancient-forest friendly. The printer holds FSC chain of
custody SGS-COC-2061

FSC
www.fsc.org
MIX
Paper from
responsible sources
FSC® C018072

# Contents

# The contributors

**Christian Amadeo** has worked in education for ten years, undertaking research and developing policy in national, regional and local government and in educational institutions.

**Dale Bassett** is Head of Public Policy at AQA, the awarding body and educational charity. As a specialist in education policy he has written extensively on the structural reform of the schools system, as well as on improving curriculum, qualifications and teaching. He writes here in a personal capacity.

**Sophy Blakeway** is Director of Education for ARK Schools. She has been the head teacher of two schools in Hampshire, most recently Hiltingbury Junior School, described as outstanding by OFSTED in inspection reports of 2008 and 2010. She has also worked as a School Improvement Partner for three schools and in 2009/10 as executive head of a school in challenging circumstances.

**Kevan Collins** is the former Director of Children's Services and Chief Executive of the London Borough of Tower Hamlets.

**Frank Field**, formerly Director of the Child Poverty Action Group, has been the Labour Member of Parliament for Birkenhead since 1979. He has held a number of positions including chair of the Social

Security Select Committee (1990–97), Minister for Welfare Reform (1997–98) and conducted an Independent Review on Poverty and Life Chances for the Government in 2010.

**Professor Chris Husbands** is an educationist, university leader, academic and public servant. He became Director of the Institute of Education in 2011; he has served on the Board of the Training and Development Agency for Schools, was a member of the RSA/Pearson Academies Commission, and has directed research projects worth over £5 million.

**Dr Tina Isaacs** is a senior lecturer of educational assessment at the Institute of Education, University of London, where she is programme leader for the Master's Degree in Educational Assessment. She is also Faculty Director for Consultancy and Knowledge Transfer and Co-Director of the Post-14 Centre for Innovation and Research.

**Michael Keating** is a freelance adviser on good diversity, equality and cohesion practice. Between 1994 and 2002 he was a councillor in the London Borough of Tower Hamlets with a number of key responsibilities for education.

**Danny Kruger** is the founder and Chief Executive of Only Connect, a crime prevention charity working with prisoners, ex-offenders and youth at risk in London.

**Dr Tim Leunig** is currently on leave from the London School of Economics to serve as senior policy adviser to ministers in the Department for Education. He was previously Chief Economist for the liberal think tank, CentreForum.

**Stephen Machin** is Professor of Economics at University College London and Research Director of the Centre for Economic Performance at the London School of Economics. Previously he has been visiting Professor at Harvard University (1993/4) and at the Massa-chusetts Institute of Technology (2001/2).

**Paul Marshall** is an academy sponsor, chair of ARK Schools, and chair of the management board of the liberal think tank CentreForum.

**Chris Paterson** is Senior Researcher at the liberal public policy think-tank CentreForum. He specialises in social policy and educa-tion, with a particular focus on social mobility. He was previously a solicitor at city law firm Slaughter and May.

**Dr Olmo Silva** is a Senior Lecturer at the Department of Geography and Environment at the London School of Economics. He is also a Research Associate at the Spatial Economics Research Centre and at the Centre for Economic Performance at the LSE.

**Charlie Taylor** was for five years the head teacher of the Willows Special School for children with behavioural, emotional and social difficulties. Since then he worked as the expert adviser on children's behaviour to the Department of Education. He is currently the chief executive of the Teaching Agency.

**James Toop** is Chief Executive of Teaching Leaders, a leadership development programme for middle leaders in schools in challenging contexts. Previously he was a French teacher in the inaugural Teach First cohort and a management consultant at Monitor Group.

**Tim Weedon** worked at the Cabinet Office on the Independent Review on Poverty and Life Chances in 2010 and is currently a Senior Parliamentary Researcher for Frank Field MP.

**Patrick White** heads Frank Field MP's Parliamentary office.

**Gill Wyness** is a researcher at the Centre for Economic Performance at the London School of Economics, specialising in research into education and skills in the UK. She has a PhD in the economics of education from the Institute of Education, University of London.

# Tables and Figures

# Acknowledgements

Special thanks are owed to Sam Talbot Rice, who played a critical role in coordinating and bringing together the multiple contributions, to Sam Tomlin, who ably assisted on background research for the introduction, and to Amanda Spielman, for her wisdom and abundant insights throughout the process in her capacity as foil, critic and quality controller.

# Glossary of abbreviations

| | |
|---|---|
| ADD | Attention deficit disorder |
| ADHD | Attention deficit hyperactive disorder |
| ARK | Absolute Return for Kids |
| ASD | Autistic spectrum disorder |
| BESD | Behavioural, emotional and social difficulties |
| BTEC | Business and Technology Education Council |
| CAMHS | Children and Adolescents' Mental Health Service |
| COP | Code of Practice |
| CTC | City technology colleges |
| CVA | Contextual value added |
| DLA | Disabled Living Allowance |
| EAL | English as an additional language |
| EBC | English Baccalaureate Certificate |
| ECAR | Every Child a Reader (literacy programme) |
| EEF | Education Endowment Fund |
| EPPE | Effective Provision of Pre-school Education Project |
| FSM | Free school meals |
| GM | Grant maintained |
| GNVQ | General National Vocational Qualification |
| HCZ | Harlem Children's Zone (New York) |
| IALS | International Adult Literacy Survey |
| ICT | Information and communication technology |
| IDACI | Income Domain Affecting Children Index |
| KIPP | Knowledge is Power Program |

| KS | Key Stage |
|---|---|
| LA | Local authority |
| LEA | Local education authority |
| LLE | Local Leader of Education |
| MLD | Mild learning difficulty |
| NEET | Not in education, employment or training |
| NLE | National Leader of Education |
| NPQH | National Professional Qualification for Headship |
| NRDC | National Research and Development Centre for Adult Literacy and Numeracy |
| OCD | Obsessive compulsive disorder |
| OFSTED | Office for Standards in Education |
| PISA | Programme for International Student Assessment |
| PBR | Payment by results |
| PLTS | Personal learning and thinking skills |
| QCA | Qualifications and Curriculum Authority |
| QCF | Qualifications and Credit Framework |
| SEN | Special educational needs |
| SLCN | Speech, language and communication needs |
| SLE | Specialist Leader of Education |
| TFA | Teach for America |
| TPA | Teaching priority area |
| TPP | Teaching priority programme |
| VCE | Vocational Certificate of Education |

# 1

# Introduction

## *Paul Marshall*

*'What a wise parent would desire for his own children, that a
nation, in so far as it is wise, must desire for all children.'*

R.H. Tawney

In 2003, the trustees of ARK[1] decided to pool our resources to
develop a chain of academies in the UK. We were convinced that
many children in Britain did not get the schooling they deserved,
nor achieve their potential. And in Andrew Adonis's academies programme we saw an opportunity to do something about it.

One of our number, Ron Beller, had first-hand experience working
in Michael Bloomberg's Education Department in New York. He told
us how new 'charter schools', springing up in inner-city areas, were
transforming children's lives. We founded ARK Schools to do the
same for children in Britain.

Today, ARK operates 18 schools (a mix of primary and secondary)
and we have plans to grow to 50.

ARK's schools operate in areas where children are predominantly
poor. More than two in five of our children are on Free School Meals
(FSM), a standard measure of whether a child comes from a poor
family.[2] Transforming their lives by providing a good education has

transformed our lives as well. Seeing children grow up able to aspire to and achieve things they could not have dreamt of beforehand has been one of the most rewarding experiences for everyone involved in ARK – sponsors, heads and teachers alike.

ARK is not alone. Britain is in the middle of a truly exciting revolution in education. Around the country, beacon schools are showing rapidly improving results. Yet some schools, local authorities and even regions are still trapped in a rut of low ambition and poor performance; and even some of the best schools are still not meaningfully changing outcomes for the bottom 20% or 30% of pupils.

This book is for the people who are still being failed by our education system. It is a collection of essays by some of Britain's leading educational practitioners and specialists, who have sought to explain why attainment remains so persistently poor for such a large 'tail' of pupils and to suggest what needs to be done. Our proposals are summarised in the 'manifesto for the tail' in the concluding chapter.

**The tail**

One child in five leaves school in England without basic skills in literacy and numeracy.

It has become increasingly common to refer to these children as the 'tail'. As a statistical term this captures none of the personal tragedy of unfulfilled potential which has blighted the lives of successive generations. But it does help to distil the argument.

As Chapter 2 shows, England's tail is fatter and longer than that of the majority of our international peers. The problem is just as great in numeracy as in literacy. But it does not have to be this way. Countries like Finland, Korea and Canada show us that the tail could be half its present size.

The working definition of the tail used in this book is those students who achieve below level 2 (considered baseline proficiency) in PISA (Programme for International Student Assessment of the

OECD) tests of literacy and numeracy. These are the children who will find it hard to progress to the qualifications they need to get good jobs, and who are least likely to find secure employment during their lives. This equates broadly to the lowest quintile of achievers at age 16. The bottom quintile at GCSE level currently comprises all those children who achieve 168 GCSE points (the equivalent of five D grades) or less.

The ambition which this book sets out is simple: instead of languishing in the bottom half of the OECD's education league tables, Britain should aim to be a top-tier country, alongside the likes of Canada, a country with comparable demographics (incomes per capita and relative inequality) to the UK, but with a tail half the size. Over the next decade we must halve the size of the tail in this country, so that no more than one in ten of pupils leave school below PISA's or any similar baseline levels of literacy and numeracy.

## Why the tail matters

Each member of the tail is an individual, and as long as the education system continues to fail any individual in the fulfilment of their potential, we, as a society, are letting them down.

The path which awaits a young person who leaves school without the minimum attainment is at best confusing and at worst grim, with a significant minority immediately entering the ranks of the jobless and probably destined for long-term unemployment.

Existing Labour Force surveys do not enable us to follow the path of the tail, as narrowly defined. However, we do have a good idea of what happens to the 40% who do not achieve five good GCSEs. If you are part of this group then there is a greater than one in four chance that two years later you will be NEET, that is, not in any kind of employment, education or training.[3] If you were one of those (nearly 4%) who had gained no GCSEs at all, there was a greater than one in two chance that you would be NEET.

Poor literacy and numeracy may also lead to crime. One in two of the prison population has literacy skills below that of an 11-year-old; 65% cannot count to the standard expected of an 11-year-old.[4] Of those who rioted in 2011 and had taken GCSEs, only one in ten had achieved five good grades.[5]

Britain also does a poor job of retrieving the learning deficit once children leave school. In 2009, more than one in four 25–64-year-olds were below what the OECD defines as minimum levels of literacy and numeracy (i.e. below level 2), compared with just 14% in Sweden, 12% in Canada and 11% in the USA.[6]

The tail of poor literacy and poor numeracy extends throughout society.

## The tail and the labour market

Reducing the size of the tail is becoming more, rather than less, urgent due to the changes taking place in global labour markets.

In 1965, the year CSEs were first introduced, just one-fifth of pupils attained the equivalent of today's five good GCSEs.[7] Over 50 years, that proportion has tripled. Undoubtedly, the improvement has been flattered by persistent grade inflation, but even allowing for this, there appears to have been a significant improvement in attainment levels. Yet Britain has consistently fallen into the bottom half of international education attainment tables, and employers, like a Greek chorus, have offered a constant and mounting refrain, to the effect that young people are inadequately skilled.[8]

In essence, the pace of change in the global labour market is continually outstripping improvements in British educational attainment. We are not alone. The OECD note that 'in the high wage countries of the OECD, demand for highly-skilled people is increasing faster than supply and demand for low-skilled workers is decreasing faster than supply'. The result, they argue, is rising inequality, with rising wage premiums for highly skilled individuals and growing unemployment or declining wages for low-skilled individuals. 'Jobs are moving rapidly to countries that can provide the skills needed for any particular operation at the best rates.'[9]

There are two dynamics at work here. At the top end of the labour market, technological change is increasing the demand for more educated workers. At the bottom end the globalisation of labour markets has hollowed out low-skilled markets to a degree and at a speed that has never been seen before.

The recession has not altered this long-term dynamic. Between 2008 and 2010 employment rates rose for the university-educated, but fell for those without good GCSEs. This was mirrored by a further increase in the wage inequality between these two groups.[10]

It does not have to be like this. In their 2008 study of the US labour market,[11] Harvard economists Claudia Goldin and Lawrence Katz show that in the first half of the twentieth century, the American schooling system kept ahead of the demand for skilled workers. As a result, the premium paid for a high school or college education consistently fell between 1915 and 1950. However, more recently educational attainment in the USA has started to lag the speed of technological change, resulting in a steady widening of the wage premium from 45% in the 1950s to the current level of over 80%.

Britain needs to replicate the educational success of early twentieth-century America, and create skilled workers at least as fast as the economy demands them. Then we will have higher rates of employment, higher rates of growth, and lower inequality. If we fail to do this the principal victims will remain those who leave school without basic skills – children in the tail.

## The wealth of the nation

Of course the implications of the skills race go well beyond the ledger of wages and employment. A more highly skilled economy feeds through into higher levels of value added, higher levels of competitiveness, attracting higher levels of inward investment, generating higher levels of tax receipts.

This is primarily an economic argument, but at stake is the prosperity and competitiveness of our society, and therefore it matters to all of us. It is an argument for our nation's prosperity.

The consultancy firm McKinsey has estimated the economic impact of what it calls the Achievement Gap as it applies to the United States, combining the direct social costs of low attainment (including crime, unemployment, welfare dependency and poor health) with the opportunity costs for the wider economy.[12] McKinsey estimated that the cost of the educational achievement gap to the USA was equivalent to a 'permanent national recession' and calculated that if the USA had closed the gap between its educational achievement levels and those of better-performing nations such as Finland and Korea (which is primarily about raising the performance of the tail rather than the median pupil), GDP in 2008 could have been $1.3 trillion to $2.3 trillion higher.

In a comparable study for the UK, the consulting firm BCG found that matching Finnish levels of social mobility (in terms of raising the educational outcomes of poor children) would add £6 billion a year to GDP by 2030 and £56 billion a year by 2050. Bringing below-average students in the UK to the national average would add £14 billion a year to GDP by 2030 and £140 billion by 2050.[13]

### Educational reform and the tail – a brief history

The British education system has always been elitist – in both the best and worst senses.

Until 1965 there were no national examinations at all for four in five children. The focus of our education system was on training up a small elite, whose school attainment was recognised first through the School Certificate (from 1918 to 1951) and then through GCE O levels (from 1951).

From 1965 onwards, lower achievers could take the Certificate of Secondary Education (CSE). However, this was part of a two-tier framework, with CSE aimed mainly at Secondary Modern pupils, and O and A levels aimed mainly at grammar and independent schools. In 1988 GCSEs were introduced, creating the single national framework we are familiar with today, but the focus was still on high and average attainers. According to the Department of Education and Science's 1987 consultation document, 'the range of attainment targets should cater for the full ability range and be sufficiently challenging at all levels to raise expectations, *particularly of pupils of middling achievement, who are frequently not challenged enough, as well as stretching and stimulating the most able.*'[14]

The focus on middle attainers became more pronounced with the introduction of school league tables based on GCSE outcomes. Introduced in 1992, school league tables have become an increasingly strong driver of school behaviour. Although there are positive aspects to this, one side-effect has been to focus school efforts (including the best teachers and the most time) disproportionately on borderline (i.e. C/D) pupils[15] at the expense of their weaker peers who can often spend their last two years at secondary school as part of a neglected rump. The focus on borderline C/D pupils has slightly diminished with the broadening of performance tables to include progress in English and maths and also Best 8 value added, but nonetheless remains pronounced, especially in schools with low inherited pupil attainment.

After the 1997 general election the pace of educational reform accelerated. As well as building on the framework of standards and targets, the Blair government began a new era of structural reform, granting a small number of schools independence from their local authorities, through the academies programme. The brainchild of Andrew Adonis, the original academies programme targeted disadvantaged pupils and failing schools. The programme has been expanded under Michael Gove to encompass most schools, creating a structural revolution in the nation's schooling, but losing some of the focus on disadvantaged pupils.

Greater school autonomy and the increased 'contestability' which comes from a rich diversity of school providers should supply a lasting catalyst for improvement. And analysis of the performance of UK academies, like US charter schools, does show improved outcomes for these schools.[16] Academies which opened in 2002 have more than trebled their GCSE scores, with those that opened in the following three years mostly doubling their scores.[17]

However, the achievements of the first wave of academies do not yet prove that structural reform is helping the tail. Analysis done for this book demonstrates that while academies generate significant improvements in pupil performance overall, this is concentrated in the 50–75th and top 25 percentiles. The effects of academy conversion for the bottom quartile of pupils are *'insignificantly different from zero'*.[18]

The other important strand of recent educational reform which is highly relevant to the tail has been the introduction of early intervention strategies targeted at children from disadvantaged backgrounds. This approach is supported by a variety of academic studies[19] into the cognitive development of young British children from different backgrounds, and enjoys strong cross-party support.

Among such interventions is the literacy programme Every Child a Reader (ECAR). In ECAR's first annual programme (2005/6), the average child gained 21 months in reading age over a period of 4–5 months – well over four times the normal rate of progress. ECAR has been rolled out nationally with government funding and there are also a number of competing catch-up reading programmes.

The other main targeted (although not specifically 'early') intervention is the Pupil Premium, introduced by the Coalition government in 2011, and which provides schools with extra funding for every child on Free School Meals. The pupil premium has not been in place for long enough for there to be a reliable assessment of its effectiveness. However, there is anecdotal evidence that the money has sometimes been used to mend holes in school budgets rather than specifically target intervention strategies for children who will benefit. Moreover, the funding is not accountable or tied to specific outcomes. For this reason, Chris Paterson proposes a reform of the system, tying it much more closely to outcomes through what is effectively a payment-by-results system.[20]

If there is to be criticism of the existing early intervention strategies, it is that they are too concerned with poverty, as opposed to attainment more broadly. The importance of intervening early is supported by a wealth of evidence showing how the gap between low and high attainers increases as children progress through school, and especially from age 11.[21] However, the right conclusion to draw from this is that efforts to reduce the tail must be even more focused on the primary and foundation stages where impact is greatest; and interventions should be targeted at all children in need of support, without an undue bias towards the poor.

Overall, while the school reforms of the past 15 years have produced demonstrable improvements in average and median attainment, there has been much less progress with the bottom tier of attainers. Dale Bassett, in a telling phrase, even goes so far as to call it 'success of the many at the expense of the few'.[22]

Perhaps we should not be surprised. If we categorise the three broad waves of reform as first, a national accountability framework (national standards and targets), second, structural liberalisation of schools and third, early intervention strategies, only the third had any specific or enduring focus on the needs of the lowest attainers.

## The children in the tail

In Chapter 2, we examine the characteristics of the children who make up the tail. Three findings in particular stand out and are worthy of comment here:

First, while poverty is an important explanatory factor in pupil attainment, most children in the tail are not poor. Children on Free School Meals make up only 25% of the pupils who leave school below the benchmark of 168 GCSE points and 23% of the tail of pupils who leave school without five good GCSEs. Over three-quarters of the tail are not poor.

This is an important finding in the light of the overriding pre-occupation of educational reformers (of all parties) with economic disadvantage.

Secondly, local neighbourhood disadvantage has as much effect on a child's attainment at school as family poverty. A non-poor child in a poor area is as disadvantaged as a poor child living in a non-poor area.

Neighbourhoods are not just a symptom of disadvantage, but also one of its causes. Concentrations of people on low income tend to suffer from poor-quality housing, environments and public services, as well as exposure to crime and anti-social behaviour. The consequent breakdown of traditional social norms not only drags down aspiration but also creates huge challenges for schools to re-establish acceptable norms of behaviour before they can deliver effective teaching and learning.

Such neighbourhood effects amount to a form of 'educational blight' – and the phenomenon is apparent not just in small neighbourhoods, but in larger towns or even regions, typically those which are in economic decline, or where communities have lost confidence in their traditional livelihoods, such as old industrial towns or coastal towns. Quite often these are communities which have not so much lost confidence in the value of school education as never had it in the first place.

The phenomenon is strikingly captured in comments made to former education minister Andrew Adonis on a visit to a comprehensive school in Sunderland in the 1990s. 'Twenty years ago, when the boys left here, they walked down the hill and turned left to get a job in the shipyard or right to go down to the mines. All those jobs have gone. They might as well walk straight on to the sea.'[23]

Thirdly, and contrary to popular perception, the proportion of children with English as an Alternative Language (EAL) in the tail is virtually identical to that in the population at large: poor white children are now, by a margin, the most vulnerable ethnic group in terms of low attainment, with low-income white pupils (as defined by FSM eligibility) performing substantially worse in absolute terms than any other ethnic group apart from travellers.

The 'problem' with white children is heavily rooted in culture. A recent Cabinet Office study of aspiration and attainment in deprived communities[24] found that at age 14, white boys had the lowest educational aspirations amongst the eight groups it surveyed (including Indian, Pakistani, Bangladeshi and Black Caribbean). National educational strategy needs to be framed with this 'cultural deficit' in mind. We need a recovery within our poor white communities of the belief in education as a means to transform the life chances of children, and even of adults. In contrast to poor white pupils, UK immigrants show some of the fastest rates of educational improvement of any OECD country. In 2010/11, four out of five Chinese pupils, and three out of four Indian pupils, achieved five 'good' GCSEs. Bangladeshi students also now attain above the national average in terms of five or more 'good' GCSEs, despite the disadvantages of relative poverty and EAL. Ethnic and cultural origin is one of the more statistically significant determinants of a child's educational attainment, but not necessarily in the ways it is generally understood.

## Challenging the culture of low expectations

Despite the importance of some pupil-specific factors, it is clear from the audit in Chapter 2 that neither poverty nor ethnicity, language, gender nor SEN give us a decisive handle on the tail. Any agenda for reform has to reside less in the targeting of specific groups than in changes to the way education is delivered, from Whitehall through to the individual classroom. And perhaps the biggest challenge of reform is to overcome a deeply embedded pessimism about what can be achieved – a culture of low expectations which extends from Whitehall downwards. We give four examples below:

*a. Whitehall*

Nowhere is the culture of low expectations better embodied than in the current national framework of standards and targets for school attainment.

School floor standards, in place since 2000, are one of the most obvious mechanisms for assuring a minimum standard for all pupils. Yet the current 'floor' target for five good GCSEs at secondary school is a mere 35%; this is set to rise to 40% in 2012 and 50% in 2015. In other words, even by 2015, the message from the DfE will be that it is acceptable for a school to have up to half of its pupils missing the national standard of five good GCSEs.

Of course for a significant minority of secondary schools with very low-attaining intakes, the floor targets, even at current levels, are genuinely demanding. A 'C' grade at GCSE is a challenging target for a pupil who comes into secondary school two or more years behind.

But this should focus attention all the more heavily on the targets we currently set primary schools. It is here that complacency is most damaging. The national standard for Key Stage 2 (when children graduate from primary school) is level 4. But level 4 is not even the standard that puts children on track for C grades at GCSE. For that you need a *high* level 4.[25] In 2011, only 74% of pupils attained level 4 in English and maths combined. So over a quarter of our children are already on track for failure by age 11.[26]

Our framework of floor standards for primary schools is also deeply complacent. The floor standard for primary schools is simply for a minimum of 60% of pupils to achieve level 4 in English and maths.

In 2011, 1,310 primary schools in England (or one in ten) fell below the floor standard. Yet it does not have to be like this: 570 primary schools had 100% success at level 4, including some schools with very high levels of Free School Meals.

The current government has injected more urgency into the battle to improve primary school standards (e.g. by steadily raising the floor standard), but we are starting from a low base. For a variety of reasons

– foremost among which are the difficulty of micro-managing small schools and the priority ascribed to young people being 'happy' at school (and the fear that this might be incompatible with hard work or high standards of learning) – governments of all persuasions have been reluctant to focus too heavily on ambitious and absolute (as opposed to relative) standards at primary school level. This has been a mistake.

More generally, political leaders on all sides have been reluctant to set 'aspirational' as opposed to 'incremental' targets for the country's education, for fear of 'political' criticism if the targets are not met. This Humphrey Appleby approach to target-setting has deprived the country of an ambitious vision for its children and undermined aspiration throughout the school system. All children have been let down by this, but especially those pupils who will end up in the tail.

A more aspirational framework of targets is set out in the manifesto for the tail at the end of the book.

### b. Local authorities

Britain has some outstanding local authorities which have achieved exceptional results for their children. In Chapter 4, Kevan Collins relates the remarkable achievements of Tower Hamlets, one of the poorest London boroughs, which in the space of eight years has more than doubled the proportion of children obtaining five good GCSEs from 25% to 61%.

On the other hand there are authorities which are trapped in a rut of low performance. There is a regional dimension to this, with significantly worse performance in the north as well as in some more rural authorities and coastal towns, and this partly reflects economic disadvantage as well as the less tangible cultural 'blight' of low expectations.

However, poverty and blight are by no means the full explanation. Research done for this book,[27] which adjusts for various measures of disadvantage in the pupil population,[28] shows a very high dispersion between the performance of different local authorities, with London authorities, notably Tower Hamlets, Kensington and Westminster, substantially outperforming their peers across the country, while Hull, Knowsley, Newcastle, North East Lincolnshire and Stoke bring up the rear.[29]

Education authorities in London are on a path of mutually reinforcing upward aspiration, driven in part by peer pressure[30] and in part by increased sharing of new and best practice between neighbouring schools. We need the dynamic which has taken hold in London to spread nationwide. In Chapter 3, Tim Leunig and Gill Wyness estimate that if all local authorities were able to replicate Tower Hamlets' success, the number of pupils ending up in the tail each year would fall from 103,000 to just 30,000.

### c. Teachers

As Michael Barber has said, the quality of an education system cannot exceed the quality of its teachers. Many of our teachers have been willing to embrace relentless reform, new teaching methods and shifting standards, as they seek to improve pupil attainment.

However, parts of the teaching profession still suffer from unduly low aspiration. A recent study by the Department for Innovation, Universities and Skills found that for many teachers 'encouraging a longer-term perspective on progression amongst pupils is (as they see it) necessarily low on their list of priorities, particularly in light of the need to focus on floor targets (i.e. the percentage of pupils achieving five A*–C grades at GCSE) on which their school's performance is judged'.[31]

Although the report found that most teachers saw encouraging pupil aspiration as a key element of their role, a significant minority fell into a category which the Report described as 'resigned', in other words 'disempowered to overcome the prevailing barriers to progression'. Two quotes from assistant head teachers give a flavour of the report:

*'Well, the problem is, they're not going to listen to a teacher*

*are they? They just look at you and think, "How can you tell me what to do? You've ended up here."'*

*'I think some people, I don't know, may have been here too long or may have lost focus and lost that enthusiasm to move the school forward and it resonates throughout the whole school and then the grades fall and that's where it stands today.'*

These are depressing observations. However, if we want to address the poor attainment of the tail, it can only be through the leadership and dedication of teachers.

Indeed, a growing body of evidence suggests that teacher effectiveness may be the single most important lever for governments and schools to pull in improving pupil attainment. Variation in pupil performance within UK schools is nearly four times greater than variation in performance between schools.[32] Indeed, the UK has one of the highest levels of within-school variation in the world.

The Sutton Trust recently published an analysis of the potential gains from improving teacher effectiveness in the UK.[33] They found that replacing a poorly performing teacher[34] with a very effective teacher[35] had a dramatic impact, especially on the attainment of disadvantaged pupils: over a school year, these pupils gain 1.5 years' worth of learning with very effective teachers, compared with 0.5 years with poorly performing teachers. Bringing the bottom 10% of teachers in the UK (equivalent to 40,000 teachers) up to the level of the average would significantly improve overall educational attainment, as measured by PISA. All other things being equal, the UK would move to being a top five country within ten years.

Given the importance of this subject, we devote two chapters to the role teachers can play in improving outcomes for the tail. Chris Husbands in Chapter 10 looks at ways of attracting good teachers to difficult schools and difficult communities and James Toop in Chapter 11 looks at the role training and leadership can play in bringing new DNA, fresh idealism and new techniques into the profession.

*d. SEN inflation*

England's Special Educational Needs (SEN) regime makes a particular contribution to the culture of low expectations. Whilst every OECD country has a special needs regime for children with learning difficulties, England sets the benchmark for special needs inflation.

The level of identified SEN in schools in England is five times the EU average, with more than one in five children (1.7 million school-age children) in the country identified as having special educational needs.[36] There would need to be something very wrong with the water for England to have five times the level of special needs of our European peers – the true explanation lies in a system of skewed incentives which encourages schools to over-classify children, as explained by Sophy Blakeway in Chapter 9.

In 2011, the Special Educational Needs Green Paper highlighted the national problem with the identification and handling of special educational needs, and the DfE has promised to replace the current SEN regime with a 'simpler new school-based category to help teachers focus on raising attainment'. However, there was no commitment in the Green paper to reduce levels of SEN designation, nor any proposed mechanism that would incentivise a reduction.

## Plugging the policy gap – the way forward

For all the momentum around the current wave of educational reform in this country, we still have a large policy hole when it comes to educating the lowest attainers.

Our country has a history of neglecting the needs of the tail and, even today, a culture of low expectations which is embedded in almost all areas of government and governance.

The policy initiatives of the past 25 years have been focused, in some respects understandably, on turning round the education system at large and recovering from the disastrous reforms of the 1960s and 1970s. The national framework of assessment and targets, introduced in the 1980s, did little to help the tail and may perversely have diverted teacher priorities away from the lowest-attaining pupils; and even the structural liberalisation of schools has to date made negligible difference to the tail. It is time to plug the policy hole.

This volume of essays provides a combination of diagnosis and prescription. Some of the changes required cannot be legislated for, such as a change in the culture of expectations. Here we need 'soft' leadership, but leadership nonetheless, from government and local authorities, in setting an inspiring vision for our teachers and pupils.

Many of the changes will be dependent on the teaching profession and on delivery in the classroom. Central government will need to resist the temptation to over-meddle; but they should be hugely focused on improving the quality, standing and motivation of the teaching profession. A glance at those countries which have led the way in improving attainment for the tail, such as Canada, does suggest that raising the quality of teaching is absolutely central to the success of the strategy.

Halving the tail will also require a programme of specific reforms – reforms to the framework of standards and targets; greater focus on foundation stage provision; reforms to schooling up to age 11; reforms to the pupil premium; reforms to the SEN regime; new incentives for teachers to focus on low-attaining pupils and for good teachers to be deployed in the most challenging schools; further investments in teaching capacity; reforms to the delivery and accountability of child and adolescent mental health services; and perhaps new types of dedicated provision for the tail.

Above all, central government will need firmness of purpose in making the education of the tail a strategic priority and seeing reform through. In its assessment of the success of the Canadian education system and that of Ontario in particular,[37] the OECD highlighted the singleness of purpose which distinguished Canada from the 'spinning wheels' which too often doomed school reforms in other countries. 'Since 2000, Canada has become a world leader in its *sustained strategy* of professionally-driven reform of its education system.'

Britain now needs that same strategic purposefulness if we are to move beyond spinning wheels and join Canada in the top tier for education performance.

# 2

# Low educational attainment in England: an audit

*Chris Amadeo and Paul Marshall*

Many international comparative studies have shown English (and other British) educational systems performing poorly in literacy and numeracy.[1] Less discussed is the persistence here of a 'long tail' that never reaches an acceptable standard even in English and mathematics, despite England's relative affluence and record levels of public expenditure on education. By the end of compulsory schooling around 40% of children leave without the national standard five good GCSEs, and around half of those, the bottom quintile, are poorly educated by any standard. This latter group has an unpromising outlook for adult life, economically and socially.[2]

This chapter looks particularly at this lowest-achieving 20%. It looks at their education trajectories and outcomes, their personal and family characteristics, the places they live, the schools they attend, and the relevant policies already in place.

First, it is important to define what is meant here by 'low achievement'. In this case, we are looking at absolute achievement in compulsory education, irrespective of all pupil background characteristics.

The OECD measures standards in reading and maths using internationally standardised 'PISA' tests. Level 2 on the PISA reading scale is a baseline proficiency level. In the UK, 18% of 15-year-olds failed to score level 2 or higher in the most recent survey, against an

OECD average of 14%. Top-performing countries including Korea, Finland, Hong Kong and Canada had no more than 10% or fewer below level 2.

In mathematics, 20% of UK students did not reach level 2, just below the OECD average of 22%. These students can answer questions only where there are familiar contexts, relevant information is presented and the questions clearly defined. Many countries do much better: in Finland, Korea, Hong Kong and Singapore fewer than 10% of students fail to reach level 2.

Relative deprivation does not explain the UK literacy problem, since the UK is ranked ninth-highest out of 34 OECD countries on this measure.[3] But the UK is nevertheless seventh-worst in terms of the performance of children from poor backgrounds. Comparing attainment levels between countries and across years has its difficulties,[4] but the evidence from PISA and the other major international comparative studies suggests that we are making little progress in reducing the numbers who reach only the lowest levels of educational attainment.

A comparative analysis of England's education system compiled by the OECD contrasts the persistent rise in domestic measures such as GCSE outcomes with the lack of progress in international measures.[5] It suggests that an over-reliance on test results in a 'high-stakes' system encourages 'gaming' behaviours, especially as few stakeholders stand to lose from the resulting grade inflation. This may help explain the apparent disconnect between international and domestic measures.

In England, low achievement can be tracked back through primary school. In 2012, 20% of children did not reach the expected level 4 in English and the same percentage failed to reach level 4 in maths. Since prior attainment is the biggest predictor in secondary school, many of this group will be in the bottom 20% of achievers in 2017. In 2011, the bottom 20% at age sixteen consisted of those who did not average at least a D in English, mathematics and their best three other GCSE subjects. This is of course substantially below the national 'standard' of five 'good' GCSEs.

Low attainment in the basics at school is difficult to remedy later in life. Adult training initiatives have had difficulties targeting those with the greatest need, and passing basic adult literacy and numeracy courses does little for a person's labour market value.[6] The importance of getting basic education right during schooling is clear.

Measures of adult literacy show that the proportion of the English population at the lowest levels in international educational surveys is high and not reducing. More than a fifth of the population aged 16–25 has poor numeracy and nearly a fifth has poor literacy, defined as below level 2 proficiency on the International Adult Literacy Survey (IALS). This proportion has persisted over time, with similar percentages in the 26–35 and 36–45 age cohorts. Many Western European countries do far better in all age bands.

Poor school outcomes directly affect young people moving into the labour market.[7] Without good literacy and numeracy, they can expect to earn less and are also less likely to find a job at all.[8] The low-skilled face further difficulties as the number of graduates entering the labour market continues to grow.[9] Employers are substituting graduates for non-graduates, even where this level of education has not traditionally been seen as necessary, leaving fewer jobs for the less skilled.[10]

Putting all of these together, we have a clear picture of an educational system which leaves around a fifth of the population poorly educated and ill-equipped for a productive adult life. This is about twice as many as in high-performing countries.

We should therefore look closely at who is in this group, to help to understand what policies might be effective in reducing the number of people who end up so ill equipped to be successful in life.

We have defined the group as the lowest achievers at GCSE, averaging less than five D grades in English, maths and their best three other subjects. As we have said, the strongest predictor of educational outcomes is attainment at the previous stage of education. In England pupil progress in English and mathematics is monitored at ages 7, 11, 14 and 16 (Key Stages 1–4). Strong predictive measures emerge early from this monitoring: a child who is weak in writing at age 7 or weak in either English or maths at 11 or 14 has a high chance of being in the bottom 20% at 16.

Since educational outcomes are so consistent throughout a child's school career, we need to look above all at the characteristics of children. The 2009 OECD PISA study found that 77% of variance in UK reading performance between schools[11] could be explained by identifiable economic, social and cultural traits,[12] such as parental level of education or occupation. This relationship was exceptionally high by international standards.

Personal characteristics that may be associated with low achievement include family poverty, ethnicity, home language, gender and special educational needs.

Family poverty (usually measured by eligibility for free school meals) is strongly associated with low achievement in Britain. Poor children make less progress at school than richer children with the same levels of attainment at entry, particularly at primary level. A poor child is more likely to end up in the tail than their richer counterpart. But this obscures an equally important point: most of the tail does not live in poor households. In 2011, only 25% of the bottom quintile of achievers at 16 were on free school meals. And conversely almost two-thirds of poor children are not in the tail at that age.

Recent analysis of the latest PISA data has also shown that in England the association between family background and reading ability is strongest at the high end of the achievement distribution and weakest at the low end.[13] This is a very unusual pattern: in most countries (including Finland, Canada and Australia) the association with family background is *strongest* at the low end of the achievement distribution and *weakest* at the high end.[14] At the low end of achievement distribution, only Finland and Iceland show a weaker association between PISA reading outcomes and family background. This suggests that English education may in fact be short-changing the more able rather than the less able among poorer children, i.e., those who are above the tail.

Turning from socio-economic measures to ethnicity, we find that about 30% of the tail in the 2011 GCSE cohort is non-white, against 20% in the whole cohort. However, this does not mean that we can assume that improving performance of non-white groups is key to halving the tail: the poor performance of non-white children can largely be explained by poverty. Once we take incomes into account, white British children generally do worse at secondary school.

Taken as a whole, the UK has done a good job of absorbing immigrants in educational terms. The differences in mean reading scores between first-generation immigrants and students without an immigrant background is all but eliminated by the second generation. The proportion of the bottom 20% at 16 who speak English as an additional language is virtually identical to the proportion in the rest of the 16-year-old cohort.[15] Only a handful of countries beat the UK record in this area.

The interaction between poverty, ethnicity, first language and achievement is revealed in the analysis of the National Pupil Database for the calculation of contextual value-added. This separates out the extent to which educational achievement can be attributed to each pupil characteristic, as shown in the table below.

The contextual value-added model analysed out the proportion of children's achievement that can be attributed to each characteristic. The coefficients in Table 2.1 show that the only ethnic group expected to under-perform white British children is the mixed race white/Black Caribbean group, and that only very marginally. White British and Irish children are significantly affected by family poverty, achieving half a grade less on average across their best eight subjects. But for other ethnic groups (except the Irish) the impact of family poverty is much smaller or even negligible. And among poor ethnic minorities, only part-white mixed-race children are predicted to do worse than non-poor white children – and not by much: by between half a grade and two grades (in just one of their best eight GCSE subjects). Furthermore, speaking another language at home predicts higher rather than lower outcomes for most children on this model: the combined

## Table 2.1 Predicted GCSE point score impact of family poverty, ethnicity and first language relative to non-poor white British children, 2010

| GCSE point score impact | Non-FSM | FSM | EAL/ non-FSM Low attainer | EAL/ non-FSM Medium attainer | EAL/ non-FSM High attainer | EAL/ FSM Low attainer | EAL/ FSM Medium attainer | EAL/ FSM High attainer |
|---|---|---|---|---|---|---|---|---|
| White British | 0 | −22 | | | | | | |
| Irish | 3 | −25 | | | | | | |
| Any other white | 13 | 6 | 45 | 33 | 8 | 38 | 26 | 1 |
| White and Black Caribbean | −2 | −10 | 30 | 18 | −7 | 21 | 10 | −15 |
| White and Black African | 11 | −3 | 42 | 31 | 5 | 29 | 17 | −8 |
| White and Asian | 11 | −8 | 42 | 31 | 6 | 24 | 12 | −13 |
| Any other mixed | 8 | 4 | 40 | 28 | 3 | 35 | 24 | −1 |
| Indian | 26 | 21 | 57 | 46 | 20 | 53 | 41 | 16 |
| Pakistani | 19 | 14 | 51 | 39 | 14 | 46 | 34 | 9 |
| Bangladeshi | 24 | 19 | 56 | 44 | 19 | 51 | 39 | 14 |
| Any other Asian | 29 | 30 | 61 | 49 | 24 | 62 | 50 | 25 |
| Caribbean | 14 | 13 | 46 | 34 | 9 | 44 | 33 | 7 |
| Black African | 32 | 31 | 64 | 52 | 27 | 63 | 51 | 26 |
| Any other black | 19 | 8 | 51 | 40 | 14 | 40 | 28 | 3 |
| Chinese | 36 | 31 | 68 | 56 | 31 | 63 | 51 | 26 |
| Any other ethnic group | 24 | 28 | 55 | 44 | 18 | 60 | 48 | 23 |

Source: CVA Ready Reckoner spreadsheet 2010: groups with fewer than 1,000 children in 2011 GCSE cohort excluded. 6 points = 1 GCSE grade in one subject. Low attainer at entry = KS2 average point score of 21 points (level 3), medium attainer APS = 27 points (level 4), high attainer APS = 33 points (level 5).

prediction in the table is negative only for high-achieving, non-English-speaking, part-white mixed-race children, who are probably few in number since most such children will have at least one English-speaking parent.

The extent of outperformance predicted for children from ethnic minorities is quite considerable, especially for non-English speakers at the lower end of the achievement range. Asian (including Indian sub-continent) and African children who speak another language at home are typically predicted to achieve a grade or more higher per subject across all their best eight subjects.

Gender is also a factor: girls outperform boys in a number of areas, but particularly in literacy. In the CVA model described above, girls are expected to achieve two to three GCSE grades better than boys (in one subject, or alternatively just over a quarter of a grade better in all their best eight subjects). However, this pattern is commonly seen across OECD countries, and the gender gap in the UK is in fact one of the smallest in the developed world. Furthermore, a narrow gap between girls' and boys' performance in literacy is not strongly associated with educational performance; among the highest-performing countries, only the Netherlands has a smaller gender gap (Figure 2.1).

Being designated as having special educational needs (SEN) is strongly associated with being in the tail. At age 11, at the end of Key Stage 2, 63% of pupils in the tail are identified as having some level of SEN, though this falls to 45% by the end of compulsory schooling. Cutting the data another way, at Key Stage 2, 44% of SEN pupils achieve the expected level in English and mathematics compared with 93% of other pupils. Attainment for SEN pupils decreases further by Key Stage 4, where in 2011 just 22% gained five good GCSEs, compared with 70% of other pupils.

However, this tells us more about the British SEN regime than about the tail. SEN designation in this country is often a consequence of under-achievement rather than a cause.

As was mentioned in Chapter 1, the scale of SEN designation in England is startling: almost a quarter of 16-year-olds in England are

Figure 2.1 **Difference between mean girls' and boys' reading proficiency point score (girls minus boys)**

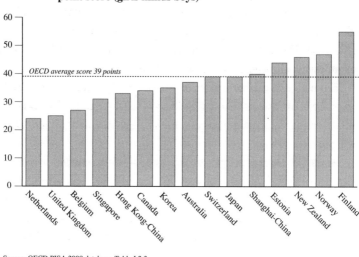

Source: OECD PISA 2009 database, Table I.2.3

defined as having a special educational need, more than four times the EU average. Internationally, only the USA and the Netherlands even come close to these levels of identifying students with additional needs. The background to SEN designations is explored in more detail by Sophy Blakeway in Chapter 9.

Family characteristics also affect a child's likelihood of being in the tail. Again, these effects are well known. Children with separated, single or step-parents are 50% more likely to fail at school, have low self-esteem, struggle with peer relationships, and have behavioural difficulties, anxiety or depression.[16] As teenagers, children brought up with just one parent experience many more spells out of education, employment or training than their contemporaries in two-parent households. For students who do not live with either parent outcomes are worse.

When families work well, they are a source of stability, teaching children how to forge positive relationships and draw support from their surroundings. Children's ability to understand and respond to the conflicts and pressures they face is intrinsically linked to how their parents deal with these same conflicts.[17] However, family structures do change through divorce, separation, dysfunction, bereavement or otherwise. These changes tend to harm a child's educational development, especially where there is inter-parental conflict.[18]

Having a child at an early age also adversely affects educational attainment for both the father and mother. This disruption tends to flow through to the next generation, lowering the child's educational prospects.

There are some other groups that are found disproportionately in the tail. One is children in care: an important group, but tiny in this context, accounting for only around 0.5% of each year group. Another group is children from traveller and gypsy ethnic backgrounds. Again, this group is very low-achieving but small – around 700 in total in the 2011 GCSE cohort.

Turning from pupil and family characteristics to wider demographic and educational factors, we next look at the places where children in the tail live, and the schools they attend.

The English policy focus on free school meal eligibility appears to downplay the importance of the neighbourhood in which a child grows up. The contextual value-added model described above helpfully separated out the predictive effect of family poverty from the effect of broader neighbourhood deprivation. Being on free school meals predicted that a white British child would achieve up to 22 points less at GCSE than a child not on free school meals. But living in a very deprived area predicts a similar or greater reduction – independently of any impact of being on free school meals. So for a non-poor child in Tower Hamlets, the predicted negative impact of neighbourhood deprivation is 36 GCSE points, about three-quarters of a grade on average across a child's best eight subjects. For the poorest super output areas,[19] the average predicted negative impact of living in that area is 26 GCSE points, independently of the negative impact of free school meal status.

The general presumption is that a school intake with a high proportion of deprived children of itself depresses educational attainment overall, with negative effects relating to anti-social peer groups, weak family and social networks, or a lack of strong role models.[20] Quantitative evidence on the extent to which neighbourhoods affect attainment is conflicting[21] but suggests some effects.[22]

But it would be rash to conclude that adding or substituting a policy focus on disadvantaged areas could be the key to transforming the tail. Schools in disadvantaged areas may be working just as well as or even better for their tail than their counterparts in more advantaged areas. The surprising findings from the Jerrim study mentioned above suggest that disadvantage factors are actually bearing least heavily on the lowest attainers. And despite common perceptions, schools with a large proportion of poor students seem to deliver the best progress for them. High levels of FSM among the student body is associated with more rapid progress for FSM pupils. These pupils do best in schools with very high levels of deprivation (over 50% FSM), or schools with very low levels of deprivation (less than 5% FSM), as shown in Figure 2.2 below. Progress for FSM children through secondary school is actually worst in schools with average FSM levels of 13–21%. So a school focus on the needs of poor children may be helpful, and there may also be beneficial 'spill-over' effects. (However, it is probably not safe to conclude anything about non-FSM children from this chart, since the spread of prior attainment of non-FSM children in schools serving 50%+ FSM children is likely to be significantly different from that of the corresponding group in schools serving fewer than 5% FSM children.)

Where an individual lives affects their likely success in education, independently of their family background and circumstances.

In general the north is losing ground to the south: London is currently the best-performing region of England, and Yorkshire and Humberside the worst. Variations in education outcomes at local authority level are even more pronounced, even between those with populations having similar profiles of disadvantage, and are large enough to

Figure 2.2   **Percentage of pupils reaching expected level at Key Stage 2 who go on to achieve 5+ A\*–C grade GCSEs including English and maths by proportion of school intake on free school meals**

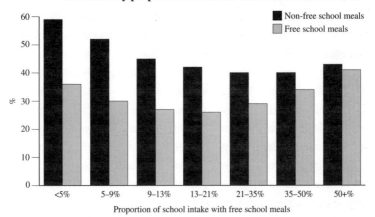

Source: DCSF, 2009

substantially affect life outcomes. Local authorities have significant input into schools, so what they do matters to attainment. Tim Leunig and Gill Wyness explore this further in Chapter 3.

Most of the tail of low-attaining pupils lives in urban areas. But children with similar levels of social disadvantage do better in urban than rural schools. Some London local authorities are amongst the highest-performing in every band of deprivation, whereas some rural authorities, such as North East Lincolnshire or East Kent, under-perform substantially relative to their level of deprivation. A study of London's apparent success shows that, when other factors are con-trolled for, the London 'advantage' begins to show at Key Stage 2 and increases gradually until the end of compulsory schooling. This suggests that advances are at least partly due to schooling, rather than simply a reflection of local population characteristics.

We can also go deeper and look at the schools that children in the tail are most likely to attend. We can take the 16.5% of 2011 GCSE entrants who were categorised as low attainers at entry to secondary school and treat this as a rough approximation to the tail. The 80:20 rule does not apply here. A quarter of this tail is found in 12% of schools; half the tail is found in 30% of schools; and 90% of the tail is found in about 75% of schools. Given that around a tenth of schools are wholly or partly selective, most of the rest do in fact have intakes that include significant numbers of low-achieving children.

The schools most likely to be attended by pupils in the tail are not necessarily high-deprivation schools. Of 356 schools with more than 50 low achievers at entry, only half have free school meal levels over 20%, i.e. above the median, while a quarter are around average and a quarter have free school rates *below* the national average of 13.6%.

There is also surprising variability in the average GCSE grades achieved by children in the tail, even recognising that the 'low attainment at entry' category covers a wide range of children. Looking at schools with 30 or more low achievers at entry, just one – Mossbourne Community Academy – achieved an average GCSE grade of a low C for this group. Nationally the average grade achieved by this tail was a low E: and the worst school averaged only a grade G. This suggests a very variable level of interest in achieving high progress for children whose results are unlikely to contribute to headline school measures.

Some, but not all, characteristics of the tail are directly addressed by existing policies.

One main policy is, of course, the weighting of school funding. We now have an explicit pupil premium. But we also have a much larger implicit pupil premium. Regression analysis of funding for all schools has shown that on average schools receive about twice as much money for FSM as for non-FSM pupils, at both primary and secondary level. So more than half of the money that goes to schools is explicitly or implicitly targeted at improving outcomes for poor children. The Department for Education has also set up measurements of attainment gaps between FSM and other children as part of its primary impact indicators.

A second lever is school performance data analysis and its use by

OFSTED, by other agencies and by school users. Published performance tables now show outcomes and progress in each school by low,
medium and high achievers separately as well as on aggregate. The
RaiseOnline analysis provided to schools and to OFSTED includes
extensive analysis of performance of groups of pupils: by prior attainment, free school meal eligibility, special educational needs, gender
and ethnicity. However, the most used performance measures in
all these analyses are based on the proportion of the school cohort
achieving GCSE grade C or better. Yet as we saw previously, C grades
are often beyond the reach of most of the tail, even in high-performing
schools.

Summing up, we know that the current policy emphasis on the
performance of groups may well improve their relative performance,
but will not necessarily eliminate English under-performance compared with high-achieving countries. For example, even if poor children were no more likely to under-achieve than others, we would
reduce the number of children achieving fewer than five Ds at GCSE
by just one eighth. While policies aimed at poor pupils are clearly
important and worthwhile, they will not on their own transform UK
performance.

This inevitably brings us back to the education system: schools,
local authorities and academy chains, teacher training, central government. And above all, what happens in the classroom. That is where
all children, whatever their abilities or backgrounds, learn – or fail to
learn.

# 3

# TOWIE: the answer to regional inequality

*Tim Leunig and Gill Wyness*

## Introduction

Britain is a geographically unequal country, exemplified by the widely discussed 'North–South' divide. The main reason why people are richer in some places than in others is not location, or opportunity, but skills. People who live in London and the South East have more formal qualifications than those in other regions. That is the single most important reason why they are better paid.

The regional skills differential is partly caused by migration within Britain. London, in particular, attracts many of our brightest and best young people, often fresh from university. There is only a limited amount that government can do about this.

Differences in skills by region are also caused by differences in school results in different areas. School results vary dramatically by area. This book is about children in 'the tail', children who end up in the bottom 20% by results at age 16. It is not the case that 20% of children in each area end up in the national tail. The best-performing local education authority is the Isles of Scilly, where no child ended up in that group last year.[1] The next-best authority was Rutland, with 9% of its children ending up in this position. At the opposite extreme, 40% of children in Hull schools end up in the tail. As we shall see, differences in parental incomes and other variables cannot explain the whole of this gap. Hull schools are performing poorly. Whatever the cause, differences like this will make it very hard for Hull to catch up with areas like Rutland in the medium term.

It is not realistic to expect that people with poor results in Hull will ever be as well off as people with good results in Rutland. If we want to reduce the level of regional income inequality, therefore, we have to reduce the level of educational inequality. TOWIE – The Only Way Is Education – is the only way to reduce regional inequality in Britain.

## Regional inequality in Britain today

People in some parts of Britain are much richer than people in other areas. The most prosperous region is London, where 'Gross Value Added' – the regional equivalent of national income – is over 50% above the national average. At the opposite extreme, Wales has a gross value added a quarter below the national average. Taken together, those two figures mean that London is more than twice as product-ive, and twice as rich per person, as Wales. Although this is the most extreme example, we know that regional inequality more generally has been increasing recently. The standard deviation – a measure of the extent of variation between places – has increased from 16 in 1997 to 22 by 2010.

This regional pattern is replicated at local level. We have good data at the 'NUTS3' level, which divides Britain into 131 places, broadly districts or cities. The richest place (Inner London – West) is exceptionally rich, three times as wealthy as even the runner-up, and five times as wealthy as the average place. The poorest place, Gwent Valleys, is only just over half the national average. Perhaps a better measure is the ratio of the tenth-richest to tenth-poorest place. This excludes the extremes, but still tells us about the scale of the income differences between rich and poor places. That ratio is about two to one – a ratio that has remained broadly stable since 1997.

There is no simple North–South divide at local level. The richest ten places consist of six in London and the South East, three in Scotland and one in Northern Ireland. The poorest ten include four places in Wales, one in Northern Ireland, and five in Northern England, broadly defined. The poorest place in the South East, the Isle of Wight, is the 17th-poorest place in the UK, while the richest place in the North, Leeds, is the 15th-richest place.

Everybody has their own theory as to why some areas are struggling and others are prospering. The evidence, however, is relatively clear: area effects contribute a very small percentage to the overall variation of wages. In other words, it isn't living in Chelsea that makes you rich, rather being rich allows you to live in Chelsea. That is pretty obvious when we think of an area such as Chelsea, but the evidence supports this contention at the broader regional level as well.

A crude way to look at this is via the ratio of people with degrees to those with no or few qualifications. When we look at Britain as a whole we find that for every 100 people with degrees there are 36 with no qualifications, and a further 102 with no qualifications above GCSE level or equivalent. In London, however, there are only 21 people without qualifications, and 53 with only GCSEs per 100 with degrees. We can see, therefore, that London has only around half as many low-skilled people as the country as a whole. London is rich in large part because it has a well-educated workforce. In contrast Northern Ireland has 97 people without any qualifications, and a further 123 with only GCSEs per 100 people with degrees. Northern Ireland is poor largely because it has a disproportionately low-skilled workforce.[2]

## School results in Britain today

'The tail' – those who do badly at school – encompasses both the relative handful who get excluded, or have particular educational needs, as well as those who just don't seem to get much out of school. How well you do is defined by a GCSE points system. We give students 58 points for an A* at A level, 52 for an A, 46 for a B and so on, and we give credit for other qualifications that are equivalent to GCSEs. For simplicity we look at how well a student does in English, maths, and their best three other subjects.[3] On this measure a student getting 168 points or fewer will be in the bottom quintile. This means that all of the tail achieves less than five Ds at GCSE, or equivalent.

As we shall see, this level of attainment does not put them in a good position either to get a good job, or to study further. This does not, of course, mean that they will never be employed, or will always be poor. There are many jobs for people with physical strength, or a good manner, and determination can get you a long way. But this group is much more vulnerable than any other.

We have already seen that there is a big divergence between the number of children who end up in the tail in Rutland and in Hull. Those numbers – 9% and 40% – are stark. More generally, there exist differences between schools within a local authority, between local authorities within a region, and between regions. The highest-performing region is the South West, where 17% of children end up in the tail. The region with the biggest problem is the North East, where 23% of children end up in the tail. The full data can be found at www.thetailonline.com. The tail is widely, but not evenly, distributed.

It is hard for social scientists to explain the GCSE results of any particular child. Some children are clever, and others are not. Some children work hard, and others do not. Some children are taught by talented teachers, and some are not. Some have supportive backgrounds, and some do not. But for all those problems in explaining the success of any one child, we can say a surprising amount about children as a whole. We can investigate the effect of gender, ethnicity, income, and so on. We find that boys are more likely to end up in the tail than girls, as are white children, and poor children.

The gender ratio is almost identical across the country, but affluence and ethnicity, immigration status and so on are not. We can therefore take these into account in comparing areas. Once we have

Figure 3.1   **How much of the tail would disappear in each area if that area met national best practice?**

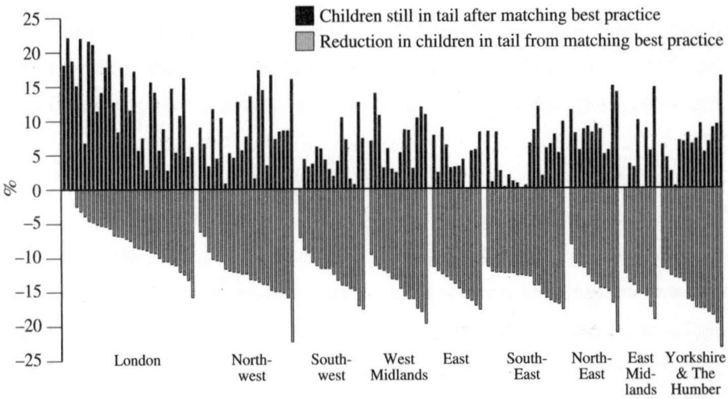

Each bar represents one local authority.
Source: National Pupil Database, DfE (2009).

taken these into account we find that the best-performing local author-ity is Tower Hamlets. Although 22% of its pupils end up in the tail, we would expect many more, given the backgrounds of people living in Tower Hamlets. Notice that we are not condoning under-performance by children from such backgrounds, simply recording the outcomes for such children. We return to the issue of raising standards for these children at the end of the chapter.

Since Tower Hamlets represents current best practice, we can cal-culate how much better children in other areas would do were they to attend schools that are as effective as those in Tower Hamlets.[4] The results are set out in Figure 3.1, which groups local authorities into regions, and ranks the regions according to their ability to get children out of the tail. The highest-performing area is London, the lowest-performing area is Yorkshire and Humberside. Notice that we take into account the backgrounds of the children in making this assess-ment: it is not based on headline results.

Figure 3.1 breaks down the total number of children who are actu-ally in the tail into two groups. The first group comprises those who would end up in the tail even if they attended a school as effective as those typically found in Tower Hamlets. The number of children in this group is represented by the black bars above the line. The second group comprises those who did end up in the tail, but who would not have done so had they attended a school as effective as those in Tower Hamlets. These children are represented by the grey bars below the line.

The graph shows us that there are three boroughs in London with outstanding performance – these are Tower Hamlets itself, as well as Kensington, and Westminster. Yet even within London we can see some poor performers. The worst is Merton, where 16% more children end up in the tail as would be the case were schools to be as effective as those in Tower Hamlets. This means that 260 Merton students ended up in the tail because Merton schools fall short of best practice.

Merton's performance is remarkably poor by London standards, but 31 of the 151 local authorities in the dataset perform worse than Merton. The worst-performing authority is Hull, where 23% more students end up in the tail than would be the case if Hull's schools were as effective as those in Tower Hamlets. Hull is closely followed by Knowsley, at 22% excess, Newcastle at 21% excess, and North East Lincolnshire and Stoke at 20% excess. These results are terrible.

The Tower Hamlets performance is the best in the country, but is by no means perfect. There is variation across schools in Tower Hamlets, and no doubt some teachers are more effective than others within even the best school in that borough.

It is of course possible that Tower Hamlets has been lucky – that its intake is 'better' in some way not captured in the data, and that its performance may drop back a little in the years to come. It may be, therefore, that Tower Hamlets is an unrealistic benchmark for what can be achieved nationwide. By contrast, it is hard to argue that any local authority should do worse than the current London average. Yet only the Wirral and Bury in the North West, and the Isles of Scilly in the South West, beat the London average.

We therefore calculate the effect of improving education in those areas that perform worse than London, taking into account their circumstances. The calculation shows that the number of pupils who end up in the tail outside of London would fall by 33,000, from 103,000 to 70,000.[5] That is a transformational outcome. If we are able to replicate Tower Hamlets' success, the number of students ending up in the tail would fall by 73,000 to just 30,000. That would be a remarkable outcome, and one worth keeping in mind when we set our aspirations for what can be achieved. All we need to do to halve the number in the tail is to reproduce existing best practice nationwide.[6]

London's success is relatively recent. This is a very encouraging signal, as it tells us that it is possible to improve educational standards in an area reasonably quickly, and thoroughly. London Challenge – whereby schools are grouped according to similarities, and told about relative strengths and weaknesses – appears to have been key. There is no reason why this cannot be replicated elsewhere.

## School results and economic performance

It is possible to do badly at school and go on to get a good job, but it is not common. The Labour Force Survey shows that in 2012 85% of people with a degree were in work, 75% of people with an A level or equivalent were in work, 66% of people with GCSEs were in work, but only 42% of people without qualifications were in work. The reality is that having few qualifications is catastrophic for your lifetime employment trajectory. And without work, poverty and dependence on benefits are all but inevitable.[7]

We noted earlier that it was plausible to believe that between 33,000 and 73,000 fewer people outside London should be in the tail than is currently the case. Addressing this issue would raise employment, in line with the figures given above. This implies around 10,000 additional jobs per cohort. Given that there are around 50 cohorts in the labour market, from age 16 to around 66, employment would, at a first approximation, rise by around 500,000 in total. This is not sufficient to solve unemployment, but it would be a life-transforming event for half a million people, and their families.

## What needs to be done?

Clearly the first step is to roll out best practice. This does not so much mean best actual practice, but best practice in terms of learning how to be an effective school. London Challenge has shown what is possible. Rather than replicating London Challenge on a regional basis, it will often make sense to have schools outside London learn from schools inside London. This is likely to accelerate the rate of learning. One head, who took over a failing primary school in a poor area, told me about the effect of visiting a high-performing school that had a similar catchment. He went back, brimming with ideas, but many of his staff did not believe what he told them. So he took them, en masse, to see the high-performing school. Two years later his school is out of special measures, and he is hopeful of an outstanding OFSTED inspection, if not this time, then certainly next time. The life chances of many students in his community have been transformed.

There remain real challenges, however. Even in Tower Hamlets, after all, 22% of children end up in the tail. The reality is that Tower Hamlets – and for that matter Hull and Knowsley – have tough intakes, and even with current best practice too many children end up in the tail. Our graph in Figure 3.1 shows that many people would still be in the tail even if we were able to ensure best practice nationally. It also shows that those students are heavily concentrated in currently poorer parts of the country. The area with the largest proportion of such children is in fact Tower Hamlets itself, closely followed by Islington, Hackney and Newham. In absolute terms the spread is much broader, with the top ten areas consisting of Birmingham, Kent, Newham, Manchester, Lancashire, Liverpool, Norfolk, Tower Hamlets, Bradford and Leeds. Here the pupil premium is critical: we need to find ways to use it effectively that go beyond current best practice.

## Conclusion

This chapter describes the regionally uneven distribution of the tail. It shows, as others have documented, that London schools outperform, and argues that replicating those standards will have significant effects on the rest of the country. That will help to narrow the gap between regions. It also argues that we need to do more, and work hard on tackling the correlation between poverty and poor performance. Unless we do that, poor areas will continue to be characterised by poor results, and those poor results will in turn entrench poverty in those areas. We must break this vicious circle, once and for all. The only answer to regional inequality is a successful education system. Education is a long-term answer, but – unlike every other answer that has been tried – it will work.

# 4

# An East End tale …

*Kevan Collins and Michael Keating*

## Introduction

Take the community with the highest levels of child poverty in the
country and place improving education standards at the heart of a
sustained and tenacious reform agenda …

Tower Hamlets is a place of contrast and inequality. The south of the
borough, once dominated by London's docks, is now home to Canary
Wharf, the financial centre of Europe. To its west lies the City, London's historic commercial heartland, and to the north the new Olympic
Park creates a regenerated and vibrant border. Move in from its fringes
and walk the streets of Whitechapel, Stepney or Poplar and you will see
that in spite of unparalleled economic growth Tower Hamlets is also
one of the poorest boroughs in the country. In 2010 the Audit Commission reported that people who work in Tower Hamlets enjoy an average
annual salary of £64,000, yet some 25,000 of the 60,000 families living
in the borough's eight square miles survive on an annual income of less
than £15,000. Tower Hamlets has some of the highest levels of work-
less households in the country – although the borough has more job
vacancies than registered job seekers. In 2010, 58% of children attending its 107 schools were eligible for free school meals compared with
the national average of 18%. The borough is where many of London's
highest earners work and where many of the city's poorest residents live.

Figure 4.1 **% pupils achieving 5 A\*–C including English and mathematics**

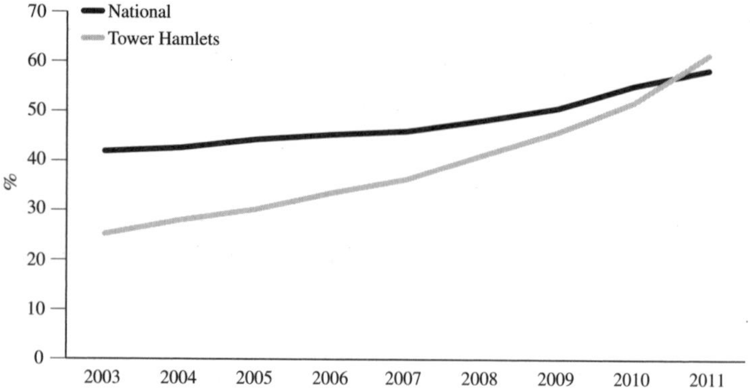

Source: DfE website, Data Research and Statistics, accessed 2012.

There is a strong and well-established link between poverty and education failure. Tower Hamlets' position as the borough with the highest proportion of children eligible for free school meals means many would predict poor educational outcomes and low expectations. However, the reality is quite different, and this is why its story is important. If the poorest children in the country can achieve, why can't all children? In Tower Hamlets, education standards have seen a long, sustained journey of improvement, with its pupils perform-ing above the national average at the end of both their primary and secondary education. Bucking the trend and securing outcomes that break the link between economic disadvantage and low standards hasn't been the result of luck, a sleight of hand or the consequence of upwardly mobile demographics. Indeed, throughout the period of improvement the proportion of children eligible for free school meals has remained constant. Progress has been the reward for sustained collective effort, hard work and a relentless and reliable focus on improving children's outcomes.

## Building a culture of ambition

Along with all London boroughs, Tower Hamlets Council became an education authority in 1990 after the abolition of the Inner London Education Authority. In that year just 8% of its pupils achieved 5+ A*–Cs at GCSE. The lack of push for aspiration was underpinned by two different but related views. On one hand was the longstanding sense that working-class children didn't need to do that well at school because the local economy could provide all the opportunities they might need. On the other was the argument that the reality of local deprivation meant young people would always fail to match their counterparts in more comfortable areas. In the 1994 local elections the ruling administration was defeated by a group of generally younger politicians including a number from the Bangladeshi community. New community groups emerged including influential parent groups who wanted to play a greater part in the governance of local schools. Notions of aspiration started to replace accepted views that local residents were simply victims of their class or ethnicity – and the focus was on local young people and their education.

By the early 1990s the changing nature of the school population meant that an increasingly large proportion of the borough's pupils did not speak English as their first language. The majority of these, although not all, came from the Bangladeshi community and were predominantly from Sylhet province with extensive family and kinship links, and were overwhelmingly Muslim. This community is also politically active and aspirational and, following 1994 particularly when it had greater representation in local decision making, began to ask questions of schools and local officials about educational achievements and standards. Why aren't results better, where are the teachers from the local community and what will you do differently if we commit to maintaining consistent levels of funding? Sometimes, of course, these questions could be awkward and uncomfortable but it was evident that this community was more ambitious about education than others had been previously.

The growing concerns of the new generation of young politicians with a strong stake in the education of the borough's children were confirmed by the 1998 OFSTED inspection report. In many ways this report provided the kick-start to a period of sustained improvement. A snippet from the report captures an overall judgment of failure:

> *The evidence does not suggest that the expenditure deployed to combat disadvantage in Tower Hamlets since its incorporation in 1990 has achieved its primary objective of raising standards. The reasons for this are complex, and the onus for failure lies with the schools as well as the LEA, but to have used resources inefficiently is doubly unacceptable in so deprived a context. (OFSTED 1997)*

Re-reading the report, it is clear that the authors described collective failure. The responsibility for low standards was shared: local politicians, schools, the officers of the council – all were judged to be culpable. However, the report also identified examples of progress and grounds for optimism. It praised the actions of the borough's newly appointed Chief Education Officer (Christine Gilbert) and suggested that under her leadership Tower Hamlets had good prospects for improvement. Presenting the failure and solution as a shared responsibility helped to galvanise those responsible for education standards and set the context for an approach best characterised as *a relentless and reliable focus on standards, standards, standards.*

A defining feature of the Tower Hamlets approach emerged as the political, council officer and community leadership established a broad consensus to challenge low expectations and place education at the centre of the Council's agenda. This commitment aligned the priorities of the policy makers with the strong and longstanding commitment to education that was deeply engrained in many of the ethnic minority communities that live in Tower Hamlets. When local policies are aligned to the aspirations and culture of the local community genuine improvement is possible.

*Accountability for the performance of local education **systems** is important. Holding leaders accountable for the collective performance of schools establishes permission and responsibility to challenge complacency and the association between economic disadvantage and low expectations.*

## The power of evidence

From the outset Tower Hamlets decided to embrace the standards agenda of the 1997 Labour government and in particular the National Strategies. The local authority emerged as a formidable implementation and delivery organisation. The focus on a core set of teaching and learning priorities coupled with a broad consensus on standards led to rapid improvement and a growing self-confidence in the schools and the local authority.

In the borough's 78 primary schools attention was unashamedly directed to literacy and numeracy. The majority of children attending primary schools in Tower Hamlets come from homes where at least one parent uses another language. For example in 2010 over 70% of Reception-aged children were classified as EAL (having English as an Additional Language). Teachers in the borough's primary schools have always appreciated that many children arrive at school with little experience of English literacy and that school will have to play the key role if the children are to become independent, self-improving learners. The schools rejected the false dichotomy between literacy and numeracy and a creative and engaging curriculum. Indeed, perhaps more than most, they knew that high standards in the basics were essential to secure access to the full range of the primary curriculum.

The big shift introduced by the National Literacy Strategy (NLS) in 1997 was the term-by-term expectations set out in the National Framework, which challenged established expectations. For some teachers the proposal that you 'teach up to the curriculum' rather than 'take it down to the child' was a fundamental issue. The borough was steeped in the whole language and integrated learning tradition. Whole class teaching and direct instruction of literacy skills was rare. The Local Education Authority (LEA) advisers encouraged teachers to plan and teach to the expected level and 'allow yourself to be surprised'. The borough's involvement in the literacy project as a precursor to the NLS provided invaluable local examples and demonstrated that Tower Hamlets' children could achieve more. This local knowledge, coupled with the authority's appreciation that implementation of the strategies secured national support to drive the transformation of its primary schools, created a powerful and irresistible culture of compliance.

In 1997, 46% of the borough's children achieved the expected level in English at the end of primary school. This figure was 16% below the national average. By 2002 the gap had closed to 3%, with 68% of Tower Hamlets' children leaving primary school achieving level 4, against a national average of 71%. Mathematics results enjoyed similar success. Just over 50% of children achieved level 4 in the 1997 mathematics test. By 2002 this figure had increased to 75%, with the gap between Tower Hamlets and the national average closing from over 11% to 2%. In 2006 the primary results overtook the national averages and have sustained that position to date. Moreover, progress hasn't been achieved by leaving a trail of poorly performing schools in its wake. In 1996 the KS2 results ranged from a pitiful 7% of children achieving the expected level to 84%, with an average at 35.6% – over 20% below the national average. In 2006 the borough average of 80% moved 1% above the national figure and with the range of performance in Tower Hamlets ranging between 58% and 96%. Lifting overall performance while narrowing the range is often described as the 'holy grail' of school improvement.

The close alignment between an established culture to tackle the disadvantage and an ambition to succeed in the national tests supported a reform of local education values and the emergence of a shared effort and accountability. This shift challenged the tradition of using poverty as the excuse for failure and transformed the culture into one of ambition, excellence and high standards for all.

*Literacy and numeracy are the foundations of future success. We know enough and have the evidence to deliver a literacy and numeracy guarantee for every child before they progress to secondary education.*

## Secondary is not the same

As the KS2 results improved, attention inevitably moved to the secondary schools in the borough. The sharp and clearly articulated literacy and numeracy strategies were set against diverse and in some cases incoherent individual school approaches. Many of the secondary schools were preoccupied with managing the behaviour of the pupils and obligations they had taken on for community services. Early in the 2000s, three approaches came together to shape the authority's secondary strategy.

- Tower Hamlets invested heavily in its capacity to produce and use high-quality data, in particular the use of individual pupil tracking to inform and drive local accountability. Using these data to set expectations of pupil progress transforms conversations from the anonymity of averages to focus on individual children. From an early stage the authority accounted for a range of contextual information to support direct comparisons between schools in similar circumstances. With 78 primary schools, the local dataset was big enough to make comparisons between the performances of individual schools. With only 15 secondary schools, local comparisons were fraught with difficulty. The absence of comparable data for the secondary phase changed with the launch of London Challenge in the summer of 2002 and the publication of the Families of London Schools data. At a stroke the cloak of borough boundaries was lifted, presenting authentic and compelling examples of success.

- London Challenge demonstrated the power of a broader city approach and the limitations of local authorities to lead the secondary agenda alone. Much of the credit for the significant progress made in the borough's secondary schools is the result of the London Challenge legacy. In particular, Tower Hamlets benefited from the support of experienced and outstanding Challenge Advisers who worked at the school level to bring fresh insights and a new drive for improvement. Their involvement as a third party creatively disrupted longstanding relationships that had in some cases become cosy and lacked edge. Tower Hamlets never saw London Challenge as a threat to its leadership and embraced the approach with many of the borough's head teachers given key roles and rightly asked to share their work and support others. The strategy thus played to the strong local tradition of collaborative partnership working.

- The national Key Stage 3 strategy provided an opportunity to shift the focus of attention from managing behaviour and administration matters to the core teaching and learning agenda. Experienced local teachers and respected leaders were employed to lead professional development on the structure and pace of lessons and the balance between subject knowledge and the development of key skills. Critically, the work was largely delivered as part of a whole school improvement strategy and required the involvement of the school's leadership. Asserting instructional leadership to place teaching and learning and pupil progress as the first priority of the school management agenda reformed many of the borough's senior management teams, with a number of outstanding teachers coming through to take on senior positions.

Consistent leadership at every level of the system is an important feature of the approach. Tower Hamlets has established new traditions, weaving the improvement cycle into the fabric of its work. For example, Year 6 classes are observed early in the spring term. Children's work is sampled and a likely KS2 result predicted. This information is used to support the deployment of consultants and others who offer additional support or to provide Easter schools and other supplementary programmes for children at risk of not achieving the expected levels. What's important is that this hasn't been episodic or the response to a year of poor results; it's a borough-wide event, not a one-off or for special cases. Again, when schools return from the summer break they receive a letter from the Director of Children's Services with an analysis of their results and a statement on how the authority will support the school's priorities. These activities maintain a culture and focus on shared improvement.

*Collaboration, competition and open access to data are powerful levers for improvement.*

## Building alliances for improvement

From when it first became an education authority Tower Hamlets Council had invested a lot of energy into building a relationship with its schools – and one that could be sustained through the inevitable crises and disputes that happen in local areas. Implicit within this was the belief that overcoming local challenges of child poverty and inter-racial and faith tensions could not be done by one institution alone. This partnership became increasingly important in the push for greater improvement. Sustaining it, however, depended importantly on understanding the dynamic between local politicians, their voters, the local authority, schools, teachers and parents, but also meant that relationships had to be flexible, confident enough to articulate problems and open to finding mutual solutions.

Building these relationships had therefore to be based on a sophisticated understanding of what was happening locally. Doing this was not just about an awareness of the diversity of the place and the people but also about its consequences. For instance, if the majority of schoolchildren are eligible for free school meals their families will have low incomes (and are likely to be in overcrowded housing with

poor health), if they are overwhelmingly Muslim there is no point
ignoring the role of mosques in local life, or if there are strong links
with Bangladesh it is likely that families may travel back and forth to
visit relations. Ensuring that children achieve well at school cannot
ignore these facts about their everyday lives. Tackling this inequality has to run hand in hand with specific commitments to improving
exam results or reading scores. A wave of innovation and new solutions flowed as new connections and relationships formed to tackle
shared problems. Critically, the focus on attainment and the demand
for evidence of impact ensured that resources were not dissipated or
wasted.

The authority to drive through the changes at classroom, school
and borough level came from this broad consensus forged through
collaborative working alliances of active and accountable partners.
The annual presentation of education results was a key moment in
the political calendar and scrutinised by a wide range of partners. The
local Education Business Partnership, a business-led charity dedicated to bridging the gap between education and the workplace, was
a full and active member of the delivery arrangements for the local
Community Plan, community groups were commissioned to improve
local representation on school governing bodies, and new relationships were forged to add effort and support to the standards agenda.
The following two examples give a flavour of how this worked in very
different ways.

- City firms were recruited to 'adopt' a school. Every Tower Hamlets
  secondary school has a major corporate partner. These aren't token
  relationships; they are longstanding, and have survived changing
  personnel and economic turbulence. Thousands of volunteers
  support pupils and in turn gain insights into the lives of London's
  children. Perhaps most important of all, local pupils benefit from
  work experience in some of the world's leading financial, legal
  and commercial organisations.
- A longstanding cultural issue in Tower Hamlets' primary schools

meant that children were being taken out of school for extended periods by their families. An examination of the evidence from the pupil-tracking data demonstrated that time missed in school terms had long-term implications and damaged the child's prospects of achieving their expected levels. The evidence was shared with key community leaders who decided to act and led a campaign against term-time leave. This work developed, with the Council funding the Improving School Attendance in Partnership (ISAP) based at the East London Mosque, working with identified families to support school attendance. The mosque used community radio broadcasts during Ramadan to convey the importance of school attendance, with the Imam's address at Friday prayers reinforcing this message. Parents were contacted through tea gatherings at the mosque, home visits and family work. In the space of three years attendance at primary schools improved from the lowest in the country to the national average.

*Harnessing the resources and influence of the community through structured and planned activity can lift aspirations and change entrenched behaviours.*

## Limitations and unexpected outcomes

The relationships that underpin the Tower Hamlets partnership approach were established in an era of strong local authorities and annual increases in funding. Funding formulas used to target resources to areas of greatest need favoured diverse urban areas including Tower Hamlets. The record of improvement outpaced national progress and the performance in other local authorities including neighbouring boroughs that had adopted alternative approaches and opted for radical structural solutions.

The borough's approach fell out of step with the shifting political response to education failure, and in particular the growth of the academy movement. Tower Hamlets had been a vanguard local authority for many of the Labour government's educational reforms and had benefited enormously from additional resources and support. Finding itself on the 'wrong' side of the policy agenda was difficult and uncomfortable. However, the school and community leaders led the charge to maintain and protect the partnership that delivered significant improvements. The response to growing external pressure to establish academies was pragmatic and confident.

The local system – with its mix of single-sex provision, Voluntary Aided and community schools, and large and small institutions – provided sufficient diversity and choice. Tower Hamlets was one of a few London boroughs able to offer the majority of parents a place at their preferred secondary school. Unlike many other parts of London there was no pressure from within the community for change.

As the external pressure to establish academies grew, the tactics employed by some of the advocates for change were ill judged and encouraged the local partnership to form a tight defensive perimeter. The desire to protect the local system from fragmentation may have inadvertently protected pockets of failure, exacerbated by a belief that the established improvement approach would succeed in all circumstances. Confidence in the approach limited the scope for radical action and had the effect of creating a glass ceiling on ambition.

When the borough began to use its powers to change leadership teams and establish alternative governance arrangements it signalled a shift in the approach. The decision to act quickly to tackle failing leadership teams and establish a cadre of executive head teachers leading a number of primary schools, and to create a Trust to take responsibility for one of the borough's largest secondary schools, encouraged a healthy renewal of the partnership. Some schools opted for academy status, others shared 6th-form provision, and a number extended their reach to incorporate Children's Centres. The change is still under way as the key partners adjust to a smaller local authority and the implications of a school-led system. Critically, the ethos, values and driving ambition of the partners remain constant, based as they are on the experience of successes (and failures). It is this collective local vision that provides the very best prospects for continued progress.

*Schools working with strong and ambitious local communities can achieve more than schools working alone.*

# 5

# Targeting intervention early

*Patrick White, Frank Field and Tim Weedon*

Immediately after the general election of 2010, the prime minister commissioned one of the authors of this chapter to conduct an
Independent Review on Poverty and Life Chances.[1] That review was
tasked with looking at the current measures of poverty and how they
might be reformed or added to so that they could better capture the
causes of intergenerational transfers of poverty. The prime minister
also asked for recommendations on how early years services could
be reformed to generate better development outcomes for children,
thereby ensuring all children arrive at school prepared for formal
education.

This chapter discusses responses to two themes highlighted in
Chapters 1 and 2 of this book: how to change the status quo whereby
poverty typically depresses educational outcomes; and how to address
the gap in achievement between richer and poorer children that
emerges at an early age.

Building on the work of the review, this chapter advocates an
evidence-based strategy to ensure that poorer children are no longer
inherently disadvantaged from the beginning of their lives. It will go
on to make policy recommendations that aim to break the intergenerational transfer of poverty.

## Gaps in early outcomes

By age 3 it is possible to observe gaps in outcomes and achievement between poorer and richer children. This is starkly visualised in the chart below, which is based on 2010 data from the Centre for Market and Public Organisation at the University of Bristol and from the Institute for Fiscal Studies.

*The data are used to divide the population of children into quintiles, ranked according to a constructed measure of socio-economic position which is based on their parents' income, social class, housing tenure, and a self-reported measure of financial difficulties. It is then used to chart the average cognitive test scores of these children from age 3 through to 16. The dotted line in the middle segment of the chart, covering ages 7 to 11, reflects that these data are derived from a sample of children from the Avon area, rather*

Figure 5.1  **Educational outcomes by socio-economic position quintile, across surveys and ages**

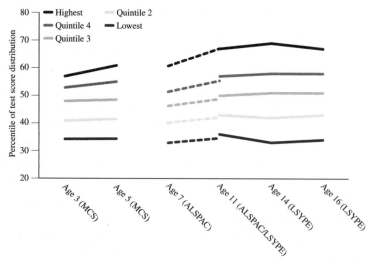

Source: Gregg, P. and Goodman, A., 2010. *Children's Educational Outcomes: the role of attitudes and behaviours, from early childhood to late adolescence*. CMPO, University of Bristol and Institute for Fiscal Studies.

*than a national sample. Data from national samples are used for all other ages.*

Poorer children begin to be outperformed by their richer peers from very early on. Indeed, differences in skill levels have been noted after as little as 22 months.[2]

Poorer children are therefore disadvantaged right from the start. They arrive at school less well prepared and less ready for education than their richer peers. These gaps remain, and indeed widen, throughout the school years: schools do not close the gap. The attainment level of children when arriving at school is therefore highly predictive of their level at the end of 12 years of compulsory education.

## The role of income

Household income is strongly correlated to childhood outcomes. Children in low-income households are disadvantaged from the start of life. They are more likely to suffer infant mortality, to have pre-school behavioural problems, to perform less well at school (as Figure 5.1 shows), to engage in damaging activities as teenagers (for example, drinking and drug taking) and are less likely to continue in education after age 16. All these factors, and more, serve to reduce their potential in the labour market as adults.

The specific causality of lack of income in promoting or debilitating child outcomes, however, is not clear-cut. Income does explain some of the gap, and money does, of course, buy items such as tuition, books and toys which stimulate development. However, studies, mostly from the USA, have shown that the effect of income on child outcomes is relatively small. Large income transfers are needed in order to promote small improvements in development levels.[3]

A useful illustration of the 'limited' influence of income is the example of children of Chinese ethnicity in England. The 2011 GCSE results in England show that, yet again, British Chinese students are the highest-performing ethnic group.[4] Analysis of the underlying data, however, reveals a number of extraordinary insights. There is a very narrow performance gap between richer and poorer British Chinese students: the British Chinese gap of 5 percentage points is dwarfed by the White gap of 32 percentage points.[5]

Furthermore, British Chinese children who are eligible for free school meals (a proxy for children from low-income households) perform better than the national average for all pupils, rich and poor, and also better than most other ethnic backgrounds, even when compared with children from richer families. In fact, poorer British Chinese children do better in their GCSE exams at age 16 than virtually any group apart from British Chinese children who are not poor.[6]

Income, therefore, clearly must be a factor which affects development, but it remains the case that being a poor British Chinese child is enough to overcome the ingrained disadvantages of poverty highlighted in Figure 5.1: while household income is strongly correlated to outcomes, this example shows that living in a home with low income does not necessarily have to result in poor performance.

If, therefore, the role of income is insufficient by itself to fully explain Figure 5.1, what else contributes to poor outcomes for poorer children?

**The importance of the early years**

Studies of longitudinal surveys, based both in the UK and abroad, show how important early life (from conception until the age of 5) is to future life outcomes.

The 1970 UK cohort study evidences that, of the bottom-performing 25% in early development scores at age 5, only 18% went on to achieve an A level or higher, compared with nearly 60% of those in the top 25%.[7] Attainment at age 7 (Key Stage 1) explains over 60% of the gap in attainment between the poorest and richest children at age 11, and the pattern is very similar at ages 14 and 16.[8] Finally, 55% of children in the bottom 20% at age 7 remain there at age 16: less than 20% of them move into the top 60%.[9]

Figure 5.2 **Decomposition of direct effects explaining the gap between children from richer and poorer families at age 11 (controlling for prior ability)**

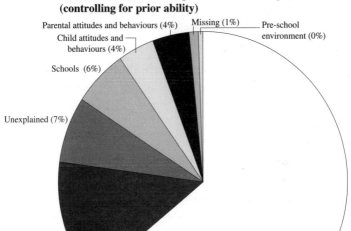

Chart does not add to 100% because of rounding down.
Source: Gregg, P. and Goodman, A., 2010. *Children's Educational Outcomes: the role of attitudes and behaviours, from early childhood to late adolescence.* CMPO, University of Bristol and Institute for Fiscal Studies.

Prior ability is by far the largest contributory factor explaining the attainment gap in the school years. After falling behind it is very unusual to catch up. Figure 5.2 shows that prior ability explains 63% of the gap at age 11. At age 16, prior ability explains 59% of the gap.[10] The age 11 gap is visualised in the figure, again based on data from the Centre for Market and Public Organisation at the University of Bristol and from the Institute for Fiscal Studies.

The early years of life are, therefore, of critical importance, and to do well one clearly needs the best possible start in life. This effectively means achieving a 'good level of development' by the age of

5.[11] Indeed, studies have shown that the successes individuals achieve during their adult life can be predicted by the skill level they have as 5-year-olds. Shockingly, only 64% of 5-year-olds in England attained this 'good level of development' in 2011, falling to 56% in the 30 most deprived areas.[12]

But, before any strategy to eliminate the gap and to tackle the intergenerational transfer of poverty is established, knowledge is needed on what determines the gap to open in the first place.

### The key drivers of children's development

The factors which affect development in the early years are numerous and varied. The best evidence available distinguishes robust associations between childhood conditions and experiences and outcomes. The consistent factor throughout is the role of parents and families: parents are key to an individual's success in life.

*Parents*
The Effective Provision of Pre-School Education Project (EPPE), an Oxford University-based early years research project, found that 'what parents do is more important than who they are', when determining child outcomes. This means that their actions rather than their circumstances are more important when it comes to influencing child development outcomes.[13]

Development is heavily influenced from the very beginning of life. The quality of brain growth, for example, is affected by a baby's attachment to its parents. By age 3, 80% of the human brain has developed. The quality of this growth is linked to strong attachment to parents. Babies who suffer both passive and active neglect can as a consequence also suffer significantly reduced brain growth.[14] Needless to say, good-quality brain development is a key prerequisite to good general development.

The 'home learning environment' signifies activities that take place in the home that aim to stimulate good development. Elements include reading to children, singing songs, and learning through play. In addition, child IQ and Key Stage 1 attainment are significantly associated with the presence of books and toys in a household. It is the home learning environment which, as the evidence shows, is the single most important factor influencing children's outcomes at age 3 and 5.[15] The home learning environment affects outcomes at age 5 even over and above parental background factors (such as socio-economic status, family income and maternal education levels).[16]

The correlation between parental education levels and early child outcomes is also very strong, explaining 16% of the gap in cognitive development between the poorest and the richest children at age 3.[17]

Additionally, positive parenting – the setting of clear boundaries and routines as well as being responsive and warm towards the child – has been shown to advantageously impact children and can lead to reductions in child behaviour problems.[18] A father's interest and involvement in the child's learning is also statistically associated with better educational outcomes, including higher attainment as well as more positive attitudes and better behaviour.[19]

Finally, despite the EPPE finding that 'what parents do is more important than who they are', 'who parents are' will, of course, often impact what they do. But the relationship between financial poverty and parenting capacity is complex. Stress and conflict, which can often be caused by lack of money, disrupt parenting. However, increasing income has not been found to necessarily promote better parenting capacity.[20]

*Child care and early education*
In addition to good-quality parenting, high-calibre child care has also been shown to be a highly positive influence on children. Attending early education provision can have a significant impact on cognitive outcomes, with those children attending for the longest time realising the greatest benefits.[21] The effects of attendance persist through

childhood so that by age 11 those who have attended a child-care facility score better in Key Stage 2 tests.

The quality of such institutions, driven by the qualification level of staff, also matters.[22] Graduate- or teacher-led early education significantly improves quality. This 'quality factor' is shown even to have an independent effect on attainment and behaviour at age 11.[23] Children who benefit from good-quality early education experiences are on average four to six months ahead in terms of cognitive development at age 5. That amounts to a 10% head start at school. Those who attended a good-quality setting for more than two years can find themselves a further three months ahead.

*Family background*

Finally, family background also influences outcomes in the early years. Basic factors, such as the number of siblings, age of the mother at birth, and father's employment status, all play a role. Cumulatively they explain 25% of the attainment gap at age 3 between poorer and richer children.[24]

Parental employment is the best route out of financial poverty, but whereas fathers' employment impacts cognitive development (accounting for one-third of family background effects), the influence of maternal employment is more complex, and has been shown to have significant benefits (overcoming any early negative effects) later in childhood.[25]

## Factors affecting outcomes later in childhood

As children grow older the range of factors influencing development begins to broaden out: their own attitudes and behaviours begin to impact attainment. Self-belief and aspiration at age 14 significantly impacts attainment at age 16 – though this is, of course, heavily influenced by their earlier performance.[26]

Parents continue to influence their children as they grow up.

Parental attitudes and behaviours explain 20% of the gap in attainment between the poorest and richest children at age 11 (and 15% at age 16), with mothers' hopes that their children will attend university having the largest impact.[27]

Teachers and schools also impact attainment. One study found that schools accounted for around 6% of the gap in attainment at Key Stage 2 between richer and poorer children, when controlling for prior attainment.[28] As with child care, teaching quality particularly matters. Indeed, schools with Teach First teachers can improve pupil performance by about one-third of a GCSE grade in every subject studied.[29]

**Life Chances Indicators**

This evidence (on the significance of the early years; about prior attainment; that schools do not close the gap; and the fact that one can predict at the age of 5 the successes individuals achieve in adulthood) shows that the level of development achieved at age 5 is of critical importance. A key question, when thinking about how to tackle poor development outcomes, particularly those achieved by poorer children, is: is it possible to use the evidence outlined above to build a strategy, focused on raising attainment, based on the proven main drivers of good outcomes for all children?

The report of the Independent Review on Poverty and Life Chances made a recommendation that a set of evidence-based Life Chances Indicators be constructed to run alongside the financial measures of poverty which are now on the statute book.[30]

The evidence presented earlier shows how life chances can be either promoted or curtailed by the actions of parents, by the quality of child-care settings, and by family background characteristics. Each of the proposed Indicators is recommended based on this evidence.

The Life Chances Indicators are:[31]

| Factor | Key elements |
| --- | --- |
| *Child-based measures* | |
| Cognitive development | Language and communication development, problem-solving skills and school readiness |
| Behaviour, social and emotional development | Emotional health, behavioural and conduct problems, hyperactivity, peer relationships and positive behaviour |
| Physical development | Body mass index and general health of child |
| *Parent-based measures* | |
| Home learning environment | Activities that parents undertake with their child(ren) which have a positive effect on their development |
| Maternal mental health | General measure of mental health that enables identification of significant levels of distress or impaired function associated with common mental disorders, such as anxiety or depression |
| Positive parenting | Warmth of parent–child relationship, and parental authority |
| Mother's educational qualifications | School, vocational or other qualifications |
| Mother's age at birth of first child | Age |
| *Environmental measure* | |
| Quality of nursery care | Quality of nursery care environment, including the educational and care processes which children experience every day, and the outcomes or the longer-term consequences of the education and care children receive |

The Indicators are all predictive of children's future outcomes, and have been chosen based on their strength of prediction, the magnitude of their impact and how well they 'corral' (i.e. pull together or represent) other indicators. The review recommended that the Life Chances Indicators should be reported on annually to evaluate progress in improving children's living environments, and that early years services should respond accordingly to the results to drive further progress in child outcomes over time.

Household income is notably absent from the Indicators, as the evidence suggests that it should be possible to mitigate the effects of low income by positively promoting what drives good life chances. Indeed, the review commissioned analysis of the correlation between the Indicators and the income-based gap at age 5. The study modelled the extent to which varying the Indicator results predicts the gap in children's outcomes at age 5, between those from low-income households and the mainstream. It was found that 'varying the [Indicator results] so that children from low-income households had levels comparable with the average for other children was found to predict virtually all of the difference in children's outcomes at age five'.[32]

The analysis further found that the Indicators all needed to be promoted 'en masse' (i.e. there is no one 'silver bullet' Indicator). The study concluded that 'no single [Indicator] was found to predict these gaps, rather, it was a result of the cumulative effect of varying all the key drivers'.[33]

Crucially, this means that the effects of income, or lack of it, are virtually surmountable. Simply providing money to poor households is insufficient if we wish to tackle the adverse factors associated with poverty when determining life chances: the policy response to this evidence should not be to concentrate exclusively on income transfers.

Instead, by positively influencing children's environments – which is presumably what occurs in poorer British Chinese households – it should be possible to ensure that poorer children can escape the circumstances of their childhood when they reach adulthood.

## The 'Foundation Years'

Services and programmes exist across the United Kingdom to support parents-to-be, children, and their parents. These services include ante- and post-natal classes, midwifery, health visitors, the Healthy Child Programme, Sure Start Children's Centres (which were established to support parents in raising their children), child-care settings, early years education and pre-school places. The list goes on.

What is more, these services and interventions can make a difference. The 'Triple P' Positive Parenting Programme, a world-renowned, evidence-based parenting programme, has been shown to improve parenting and reduce child problem behaviour.[34] EPPE, as noted earlier, has found that high-quality child care and pre-school provision leads to better child outcomes, and programmes such as the Family Intervention Services can avert the need for more intensive help for families later on.[35]

However, for a number of reasons, services are not provided effectively or consistently. Services on the ground are variable, and too often there is little understanding of outcomes achieved by or expectations of the services, or indeed of whether services actually reach the families that need them most.

All too often, unfortunately, poor families get the worst deal from early years public services. As OFSTED notes in its 2010–11 annual report, 'the difference in the quality of provision between providers in the most deprived areas and the least deprived areas remains too large'.[36] Similarly, take-up of services is lower for disadvantaged children, though this is partly a reflection of cost. In households with an average income of less than £10,000, 79% of children take up their free early education entitlement, compared with 97% of households with incomes of more than £45,000 per year.[37]

Further, Sure Start has arguably not met its expectations. Little direction is given to the outcomes expected of children who attend Sure Start Children's Centres, and assessments show mixed results, though more established centres have more positive effects.[38]

Research conducted by the National Evaluation of Sure Start research team, based at Birkbeck, University of London, compares two sets of families who did and did not attend Sure Start Children's Centres. Their study found that while the number of positive effects of centres surpassed the number of negative effects, 'the number of outcomes where there were no differences between the two samples [exceeded] both put together'.[39] Furthermore, despite these centres being established to support the development of children, the study found that, 'only in the case of physical health did children apparently benefit directly' (and physical health was only one of eight outcomes measured).[40] One might also question whether we should tolerate negative effects at all.

Reviewing this evidence, coupled with the child development statistics, it is not difficult to reach the conclusion that existing budgets could be spent much more effectively to improve child outcomes. Budgets for 0 to 5-year-olds come from different sources, though essentially these budgets can be split into income transfers and spending on services.

In the last ten years of the previous Labour government, £150 billion was spent on income transfers to poorer households.[41] Over the same period £10.8 billion was spent building up Sure Start Children's Centres.[42] Spending totals for 2010 have been estimated at about £27 billion, of which about £12 billion was spent on cash benefits and tax credits, and about £14 billion on services (Sure Start, maternity services, and child-care entitlements etc.).[43] An additional £1.2 billion was spent on child-care financial support.

These are not insubstantial figures, and much could be achieved with this level of available spending. But if we accept that the way to eliminate the intergenerational transfer of poverty is to promote better outcomes in the early years, what action can be taken to ensure all children achieve a good level of development by age 5?

The fundamental importance of the early years needs to be recognised in our services' infrastructure. We need both a cultural shift in approach and radical reform of service delivery. The establishment of the 'Foundation Years' as a new pillar for our education system, covering the early years, should bring together the currently diverse and independent sectors which at present provide services for the under 5s and their parents. Services need to become more effective and self-reinforcing. No longer should midwifery services be provided independently of health-visitor services, or of child-care provision, or indeed of Sure Start Children's Centres. Instead, a new approach should take as its core the need to promote good development in children under 5 (i.e. improvements in the Life Chances Indicators) and make policies with the sole aim of improving development levels.

We all have an interest in children achieving their best possible outcomes, and this approach should be led by central government. The current dispersed responsibilities should be pooled into one central department responsible for the health, well-being and education of our young children.

The key to any successful reform is that it answers the needs demonstrated by the evidence. Services should be built on programmes that have strong evidence bases underpinning them: for example, Triple P and the Family Nurse Partnership programme. The Foundation Years must learn from past policies and programmes, replicating their strengths and avoiding their weaknesses. The evidence presented in this chapter shows that parents are the key to success, and therefore services should engage with parents and build their skills based on their strengths. It also shows that child care is best when it is of the highest quality. The government should establish an initiative for the Foundation Years similar to Teach First. With effort and resources directed at the right places we could be much more successful in promoting the life chances of children.

Any new system must be universal, in order to avoid stigmatising some parents, but must also provide the most support to those who need it. Only then will real progress be made in tackling the income-based development gap. There are various mechanisms one can employ to achieve this, through the setting of targets, using a 'payments by actual results' model, or by looking again at the funding streams and the ring-fencing decisions made. Furthermore, hard decisions need to be taken with respect to traditional services which are ineffective at promoting good outcomes for children: such services should be discontinued.

Most important, however, is the need for a single service. Parents and their children should no longer have to navigate a range of different services from a range of different providers. It should be made easier for parents to raise their children as best they can.

## Conclusion

The evidence is clear. Early life development is critical to future life chances.

Gaps in outcomes between richer and poorer children emerge early in life and widen during childhood. Right from the start poorer children are therefore disadvantaged, debilitating their educational attainment and achievements in life: they never catch up with their richer peers. Importantly, while the gap emerges along class lines, the evidence is equally clear that income itself does not fully explain why the gap emerges in the first place. The example of British Chinese children shows that it is possible to overcome the disadvantages that poverty habitually has brought for educational attainment.

The potential for improving children's life chances is enormous. The downside is that there is a very narrow window in which to work. The evidence exists on what drives good life chances. Although a range of factors impact on development in the early years, the consistent factor throughout is the role of parents and families. But while the evidence stacks up, we remain, as a country, behind the curve in translating evidence into effective public policy.

This chapter has argued for a strategy to prevent the gap emerging in the first place. It is a twofold programme. Firstly, to establish the Life Chances Indicators to measure what we know drives good outcomes in the early years. Secondly, to radically reform early years services to build the 'Foundation Years' as a new pillar in our education system. By coalescing all services for under 5s, the 'Foundation Years' will promote improvements in children's, and particularly poorer children's, development before that age. By positively influencing the key factors that shape children's life chances we can ensure poorer children no longer grow up to automatically become poor adults.

The economic case is overwhelming. The financial cost of inaction has been estimated at between £11.6 and £20.7 billion through unemployment, ill health and criminality.[44] The moral case, of course, is obvious and requires no further justification.

What is clear, however, is that if we do not act we will continue to see poorer children under-achieve. Too many children will continue to hit age 5 without the skills to guarantee, as far as is possible, the best life possible, and we will continue to see generations of poor children grow up to remain poor in adulthood. That is not fair, not logical, and not necessary.

# 6

# Taking it as read: primary school literacy and the pupil premium

*Chris Paterson*

*'How can a child start secondary school unable to read with confidence? That is a basic building block of a good education and no child should begin the race so far behind the starting line.'*

Nick Clegg[1]

The subject of this book is England's educational 'tail': the large group of pupils who leave school lacking basic skills, facing significant barriers to full participation in society. As recognised in Chapters 1 and 2, the national failure to achieve sufficient levels of literacy is one of the most important factors – if not *the* most important – at the heart of this phenomenon. In turn, the transmission of impoverished literacy is also central in perpetuating intergenerational patterns of disadvantage.

This chapter therefore focuses on the specific issue of primary school literacy and looks to link it to the government's flagship policy for tackling disadvantage and underachievement: the pupil premium. It seeks to suggest a policy lever that would operate to emphasise the crucial importance of early literacy and incentivise primary schools to act accordingly. In doing so, it would also introduce a modest form of accountability mechanism in relation to the expanding pupil premium allocated to these schools.

## The cost of poor literacy

The social and economic costs of national educational underachievement generally have been set out in detail in Chapter 1. However, the costs of impoverished literacy specifically are equally striking.

The impact on the individual is profound from an early age. Reading and writing are prime communication skills and crucial for a child's intellectual, social and emotional development.[2] Even after controlling for disadvantage and general cognitive ability, poor literacy remains strongly linked to behavioural and emotional difficulties.[3] Of children entering secondary schools with severely impoverished literacy skills, less than 2% will achieve five good GCSEs (against around 65% nationally).[4] The same children are over four times more likely to truant and five times more likely to be excluded from school.[5] According to one study, children who are excluded from school have a suicide rate 19 times the national average by the time they reach 24.[6]

In adult life, *one in every five* people in the UK is deemed 'functionally illiterate' – defined by UNESCO as the failure to meet the minimum level of literacy required for effective participation in society.[7] One in six has literacy levels below those expected of an average 11-year-old.[8]

Simply put, those with the lowest levels of literacy are the least likely to be employed.[9] They are also, in turn, more likely to suffer from a range of negative health outcomes (from depression to obesity) and to be involved in crime (with around half of the prison population suffering from literacy difficulties).[10] Indeed, one recent US study concludes that communication disability will be the number one 'public health challenge for the twenty first century'.[11]

The cumulative societal impact of these interacting individual factors is staggering. The World Literacy Foundation estimates that poor literacy alone costs the UK economy as much as £81 billion per year (almost 4% of GDP).[12] A more rigorously costed projection by KPMG – seeking to include only readily quantifiable costs – puts the total figure at around £2.5 billion annually (including £1.7 billion in lost tax revenues and benefits).[13] Inevitably, calculations of this nature are laden with imprecise assumptions and estimates. Nonetheless, the basic point is obvious.

There is a risk, however, in this intensely rationalised and pragmatic focus on large-scale collective economic consequences that something of fundamental force is lost. It must also always be remembered that basic literacy is a recognised human right – it is, in short, a *moral* issue as well as a financial one.[14] Indeed, it is vital to realise that, for many, 'addressing literacy skills is a key first step in beginning to address and overcome other related factors that lock individuals into a cycle of disadvantage'.[15]

## The pupil premium

*Purpose*
The pupil premium sits at the centre of the government's social mobility strategy. Under this scheme, additional funding is earmarked for and 'attached' to individual children from disadvantaged backgrounds (as designated by free school meal [FSM] status). Each year, both primary and secondary schools receive this additional sum for each FSM pupil enrolled, with the express intention that it *benefit the specific child to whom it is assigned*:

> *The Government believes that the Pupil Premium, which is*
> *additional to main school funding, is the best way to address the*
> *current underlying inequalities between children eligible for free*
> *school meals and their wealthier peers by ensuring that funding*
> *to tackle disadvantage reaches the pupils who need it most.*[16]

As a result, Britain's schools are to become, as Michael Gove puts it, the 'engines of social mobility' that break the 'cycle of inequality'.[17] The links of intergenerational disadvantage are to be severed by connecting additional funding directly to disadvantaged children themselves – 'because the extra funding follows the child, it will ensure that deprivation funding is far better targeted.'[18] As the new minister of state for schools, David Laws, has put it:

> It would ... be a terrible mistake to think that the main purpose of the pupil premium is to protect schools from cuts. Its real purpose is to help lift the educational performance of pupils from disadvantaged backgrounds, so closing the shameful gap in life chances in our country.[19]

*Level of funding*

The pupil premium for the 2012–13 academic year is £600 for every eligible pupil. This will rise to £900 for 2013–14 and will likely increase to over £1,000 for 2014–15 in line with the doubling of the total pupil premium 'pot' to £2.5 billion. Indeed, the Sutton Trust anticipates that the premium for 2014–15 could reach as high as £1,750 per FSM pupil.[20] Thus, in relation to primary education specifically, a school that educates a pupil premium child for the full seven years will, from 2014–15, receive between £7,000 and £12,250 in funding for the express purpose of benefiting that child.

**The current state of literacy in primary schools**

The minimum expected level of literacy for pupils leaving primary school is defined as level 4 in English at Key Stage 2 – in effect, the level the government considers the minimum required to be able to access the secondary curriculum. Those failing to achieve this are in great danger of being cut adrift: as Sarah Teather puts it, 'being able to read fluently by the end of primary school is essential. Without these skills children fall further behind in their education.'[21]

In 2011, around 100,000 pupils – 19% of the year group – left primary school without the minimum expected level of literacy.[22] Around 35% of these 100,000 failing pupils were eligible for free school meals (and thus the pupil premium) as compared with around 18% of the year group as a whole. FSM pupils are more than *twice as likely* to fall below the minimum literacy standard as their more affluent counterparts. Indeed, *one in every three* children that the pupil premium is intended to benefit leaves primary school without basic level 4 literacy. Of these, less than 7% will go on to achieve five good GCSEs. This must be addressed as a matter of urgency.


## Proposed government initiatives: the policy context

Recognising precisely this point, the government has begun to explore positive initiatives to tackle the significant literacy problems facing disadvantaged pupils at this key transitional point between primary and secondary school. In July 2012, it announced that £10 million of pupil premium money is to be given to the Education Endowment Foundation (EEF) to rigorously evaluate 'what works' at this age in terms of remedial literacy interventions.

This initiative stems in part from the recognition that the intensive remedial literacy intervention given prominence under the previous government, Every Child a Reader, was – while effective – 'expensive', at £2,600 per pupil per year.[23] The EEF is therefore likely to focus particularly on initiatives that can provide strong results at a lower cost (potentially up to a maximum of around £1,000–£1,500 per pupil).

The intention is that the EEF best-practice guidance should be in place for the 2013–14 academic year, so that it can be used by secondary schools to identify the most effective programmes to help those 'struggling Year 7s from deprived homes ... who leave primary school without level 4 literacy.'[24] Some secondary schools may choose to begin these initiatives as part of the new programme of 1–2 week summer schools for disadvantaged pupils. However, it is clear that the vast majority of the implementation of the approved remedial literacy interventions will take place during Year 7 itself (and will be required to be funded as such). Here, secondary schools may take some advantage of the recently announced 'catch-up premium' for all children who fail to attain level 4 in Key Stage 2 literacy and/or maths – capped at £500 per pupil.

## Potential policy problems

### Accountability and the pupil premium

There is an inherent tension at the heart of the pupil premium policy between the ethos that drives its implementation and the rationale for its existence. As part of the desire to devolve power, the government has been extremely vocal about the fact that – rightly – it will not dictate to schools how pupil premium money should be spent. Instead, schools are to be given full licence to spend the premium 'as they see fit': 'We'll prove that teachers do best when Whitehall steps out of the way.'[25] At the same time, however, the policy will also involve the annual distribution of £2.5 billion of public money – in a period of severe economic restraint – in relation to a single, clearly defined purpose: closing the attainment gap by benefiting the children in question. The result is – as recognised by numerous commentators – a significant problem of accountability.

The government has sought to take steps to address this issue through the introduction of 'soft' accountability measures: schools are to be required to publish pupil premium spending information online (for 'parents and others') and a new measure has been added to school performance tables relating to the specific performance of FSM pupils.

However, there remains a clear sense that the tension has not yet been suitably resolved.[26] The current measures do not appear to have sufficient teeth in relation to such significant spending (and such an important purpose) and there are real concerns over the level of success of the initial round of pupil premium allocation. A recent report by the Sutton Trust paints a bleak picture, identifying large proportions of teachers who are unaware of how the money should best be spent and what should be prioritised.[27]

Indeed, recent findings from OFSTED indicate that the pupil premium is having little or no discernible impact in the majority of schools.[28] Rather than being reserved for its intended purpose, pupil premium money is, in general, simply being used to 'top up' the general funding pot (potentially even being diverted to 'tarmacking playgrounds' or 'fixing the school roof').[29] With this, in one fell swoop, the entire rationale for the policy is completely undermined – the defining linkage between additional funding and the disadvantaged child is severed and the potential for enhanced results through targeted deprivation funding is lost.

As the new minister of state for schools has noted, 'schools which fail to use the premium to close the performance gap, or who use the money ineffectively, must be held to account.'[30]

*Incentives and primary school literacy*
There is also a potential problem in relation to the future implementation of remedial literacy programmes following the result of the EEF evaluation, and it relates to the incentive structure likely to be in place.

Indeed, this danger already exists to some extent prior to the new policy initiatives in the area. As the KPMG analysis clearly identifies, the direct costs of the failure to achieve basic levels of primary school literacy do not actually fall on primary schools themselves.[31] It is in fact only at the secondary school level that the contingent costs of impoverished literacy – through disruptive behaviour, truancy, exclusion and other factors – outweigh (and soon dwarf) the outlay that would have been required to prevent the deficit emerging in the first place:

> *Within education, the costs of literacy failure are greater in the secondary phase than they are in the primary phase. The costs to primary schools of providing intervention outweigh the immediate benefits. This suggests that in economic terms it may be difficult to persuade primary schools to shoulder the full costs of intervention without targeted top-up funding.*[32]

There is a risk, therefore, that – despite best intentions – the current proposed policy landscape could actually exacerbate rather than address this problem, potentially increasing inefficiencies. The currently envisaged structure is that the EEF guidance will be used by *secondary schools* to choose remedial literacy interventions for 'struggling Year 7s from deprived homes'.[33] For FSM pupils, these interventions are likely to be funded by a combination of the pupil premium budgets allocated to these *secondary schools* (thus precluding other uses) and the separate specific 'catch-up premium' granted to secondary schools.[34] In effect, a structural expectation will be created whereby the responsibility for (and costs of) the failure of a pupil premium child to attain the basic minimum level of literacy at primary school will fall (and be anticipated to fall) exclusively on the secondary school.

There is a clear danger here of an incentive trap that also ties directly back into the problem of accountability discussed above. Not only will the relevant costs not fall on the primary school, but that school will have the subconscious safety net of knowing that, particularly in relation to pupil premium children, specific policy initiatives (and specific funds) are in place whereby the relevant secondary school will be expecting to pick up the tab for a remedial literacy programme.

There is therefore a real risk that – in an entirely subconscious way – literacy in primary schools, particularly in relation to the pupil premium, may even be allowed to slide further or be seen as *less* of a priority precisely because of the structure of incentives and expectations in place. As is strikingly obvious from the evidence above, this is precisely the *opposite* response to that required. The single most beneficial step in aiding pupil premium children to bridge the gap to their more affluent counterparts – the very rationale for the policy – would be an enhanced and intensified focus on literacy skills *in primary schools*.

## Policy proposal

The remainder of this chapter seeks to propose a policy lever that would operate to address (in some degree) both of these issues simultaneously by providing a modest, results-based accountability measure for primary school pupil premium spending while also attempting to align the incentive structure to ensure that literacy attainment among pupil premium children (and hopefully, by extension, all children) is made an absolute priority.

As outlined above, from 2014–15, a primary school that educates a pupil premium child for the full seven years will receive between £7,000 and £12,250 in funding for the express purpose of *benefiting that child*. If the pupil premium budget continues to grow (as envisaged by some in government), this figure could be even higher.[35] The question then becomes, in light of this, is it acceptable that one in every three of these children eligible for the pupil premium should continue to leave these primary schools without the basic minimum expected level of literacy? Is it then also acceptable to place the responsibility, expectation and onus to pay for remedying this failure exclusively onto *secondary schools*, despite the inefficient incentive structure this potentially creates?

As an alternative approach, this chapter proposes that a sum of up to a maximum of one year's pupil premium allocation given to a primary school to benefit a disadvantaged child should be made contingent on that child attaining basic level 4 literacy at Key Stage 2. Within the range identified above, that means a maximum of between £1,000 and £1,750 out of between £7,000 and £12,250 (a little over

10%). This sum would be provided to schools as part of the regular pupil premium allocation but would be recoupable if the specific target is not met – in effect, a very basic, partial form of payment by results would be introduced into the system.

However, the driving purpose behind this policy would *not* be punitive – it would not be to blame 'bad' schools or teachers. Instead, it would be actively positive. Should a pupil premium child fail to attain this minimum literacy level, the contingent sum would be passed directly to the relevant secondary school which *must* then use it to fund participation by the relevant child in one of the remedial literacy interventions endorsed by the EEF evaluation.[36] With this, *every* pupil premium child failing to reach the minimum expected literacy level would automatically be entitled to participate in a programme designed to prevent them being left behind.

Secondary schools would be completely free to choose any of the interventions deemed to be sufficiently successful by the independent EEF review. If the cost of the intervention chosen is below the pupil premium allocation for the year in question, the remainder of the contingent sum would be returned to the primary school; if the cost of the intervention selected were to exceed that year's pupil premium allocation (although this is, as discussed above, very unlikely), the secondary school could itself choose to pay any top-up fee. As such, none of the money repaid by the primary school goes to any other use than *remedying the literacy deficit faced by the child in question*.

The aim would be to refocus firmly on what the pupil premium actually is – a form of bonus payment designed not to augment the general pot but for the specific purpose of aiding the child to whom it is attached. Indeed, in one sense, the money does not really 'belong' to the school but to the child (in that they are entitled to the benefit of it) – the former has simply been given the responsibility of spending it on the latter's behalf. The school is, in a sense, holding and using it on trust.

This policy would serve to inject a minimal level of 'hard' accountability into the process of pupil premium spending in primary schools.

At the same time, it is also a policy that would be intended to operate in a way that reduces the need for its own enforcement. By altering the proposed structure and *aligning the costs of remedying literacy difficulties among primary school FSM children with the primary schools themselves*, these institutions would be directly incentivised to make better and earlier use of the additional resources being provided to prevent problems escalating. Literacy attainment would thus be placed at the very heart of primary school pupil premium spending. In turn, secondary school pupil premium allocations would be reserved for tackling the challenges of the secondary school curriculum, and the proportion of the 'catch-up premium' earmarked for FSM pupils could be redeployed to benefit disadvantaged children in other ways.

## Potential issues for further consideration

The proposed policy initiative above would, as ever, require detailed consideration of a number of practical issues and challenges before it could be successfully implemented. Although it is not possible to explore them fully in a chapter of this length, some of the main points are identified and discussed briefly below. The crucial point would be to initiate a controlled and rigorously evaluated trial to ensure that the outcomes do in fact map out as desired without significant unintended and undesirable consequences.

### Children moving between schools
The above outline assumes – for the sake of simplicity – a scenario where the FSM child in question has remained at the same primary school for the full seven years. This is not, of course, always the case in reality. It would therefore be necessary to consider how the policy would operate in relation to a child who has attended more than one primary school. The fairest mechanism would be simply to pro-rata the contingent sum in direct relation to the proportion of time spent at each school.

### *SEN status*

Significant thought would need to be given to the issue of how the policy would work in relation to pupils with severe special educational needs and the extent to which a carve-out should be applied such that the claw-back mechanism would not operate in relation to children in particular situations. Clearly there will be cases where a pupil's individual medical circumstances preclude reaching level 4 literacy and other factors may also be taken into consideration. However, it is very important that the bar is not set too low (as identified in Chapter 9). Pupil premium funding supplies the express opportunity to provide tailored or intensive support for those with particular difficulties, and a culture of high expectations and belief is central to improving outcomes for disadvantaged children (as outlined in Chapter 4 in relation to Tower Hamlets).

### *School management of pupil premium money*

The practicalities of schools 'repaying' a limited amount of pupil premium money would need to be addressed (as, in many cases, the money in question will already have been spent). In reality, the policy is likely to require primary schools to develop a limited reserve pool based on the anticipated number of failures (drawing on the patterns of previous years). One advantage of this is that schools would be able to monitor closely their (hopefully) increasing success rates each year and therefore gradually reduce the size of the reserve.[37] However, the overall mechanics of how this process would work require thorough consideration.

### *Interaction of incentives*

While the policy proposal above is in part designed to remedy a potential problem with the current incentive structure, it would also be necessary to monitor whether it could itself give rise to other unwanted consequences. For example, it would be important to ensure that there is not a hugely disproportionate impact on non-FSM children or on performance in other areas of the curriculum (such as numeracy).

Strict focus would also be required to monitor and avert the possibility of exploitative 'gaming' by schools to avoid the potential repercussions (e.g. by 'encouraging' struggling pupils to stay away from school on the day of the test).

*Best practice for literacy teaching in primary schools*
Realigning the incentive structure to increase primary school accountability for literacy in primary schools would also have the important effect of concentrating minds on what really works pedagogically *at this stage*. Rather than focusing exclusively on the most effective remedial interventions for Year 7s (which will of course remain important), considerable attention would also need to be given to best practice in literacy teaching throughout primary school itself (with a view to ensuring these later interventions become *less* rather than *more* necessary). This approach would bring with it the well-recognised benefits (both in terms of individual development and overall cost) of the early intervention mantra given prominence throughout the government's wider social mobility strategy.

## Conclusion

Impoverished literacy in early life is a defining feature of England's underperforming educational 'tail'. This chapter has therefore sought to pursue a direct link between primary school literacy and the government's flagship policy for tackling underachievement and disadvantage: the pupil premium. In particular, it has identified two potential problems: one concerning accountability and the pupil premium and the other relating to the incentive structure set to accompany the implementation of sorely needed remedial literacy interventions. It has therefore proposed the development of a policy lever designed both to introduce a limited form of pupil premium accountability and also to incentivise schools to put literacy where it belongs: at the very epicentre of the attempt to counteract underperformance and deprivation among primary school children.

# 7

# School structure, school autonomy and the tail[1]

## Stephen Machin and Olmo Silva

## Introduction

The idea that different school structures and degrees of autonomy can improve standards is one that has become popular in some quarters. What is more, some of the newer school structures – like academy schools in England, charter schools in America and free schools in Sweden – often have a preponderance of 'tail' students. Thus it is natural to ask whether there is scope for different school structures – and the differing degrees of autonomy associated with them – to alleviate the tail by raising standards.

These issues form the focus of this chapter, where we ask what can be said about this extremely important aspect of education policy by looking at the most convincing and up-to-date research evidence. We try to identify situations where evidence points to a beneficial impact on pupils in the tail of the achievement distribution, and assess whether we can find scope for these alternative institutional arrangements to work in English schools. In doing so, we will revise both the theoretical arguments and the empirical evidence on the effects of alternative school arrangements and autonomy on students in the tail of the ability distribution. To begin with, we will discuss why more autonomous school structures could have an impact on students' attainment and school composition. We will then discuss in more detail the nature of school structures in England, and place academies in this context. We will finally review some related empirical evidence coming from England, the US and Sweden.

## School autonomy and alternative school structures: why should they work?

Partly motivated by the inconclusive evidence on the effectiveness of resource-based interventions (Hanushek, 2003), governments around the world tend to favour policies based on accountability, autonomous school structures, and choice in the 'schooling market' to improve standards. The rationale for this focus rests with the idea that more autonomy and flexibility in school arrangements, coupled with quasi-market incentives, can spur teaching innovation and address low achievements. But what are the main 'ingredients' of models of education centred on autonomy and choice?

Accountability lies at the heart of these modes of schooling provision. In these settings, pupils are assessed on the basis of standardised examinations and this allows parents and policy makers to identify good and bad schools, impose sanctions and targets, and undertake closure and restructuring. Crucially, within an accountability framework, standardised tests are made publicly available via league tables to all potentially interested 'stake-holders', i.e. parents, practitioners and government analysts. This implies that schools are accountable not only to the local governments or other funding bodies – e.g. the 'sponsor' in the case of some of the English academies – but more widely and directly to parents, who can 'shop around' for school quality (Tiebout, 1956). All in all, the scope of accountability is to gather and spread information about school achievements and to allow monitoring of education progress and teaching staff performance.

Accountability by itself may provide sufficient incentives for schools to improve performance. This could occur because of 'name-and-shame' mechanisms, or through specifically targeted interventions aimed at addressing problems identified by the gathering of information. Accountability might also raise teacher and pupil motivation, and increase parental involvement in their child's education. However, it is generally argued that accountability will produce most of its effects when coupled with mechanisms that: (1) increase parental choice; and (2) grant schools some autonomy to restructure their governance and respond to the competitive pressures introduced by parental choice.[2]

Why should school choice and autonomy spur better educational standards? Arguments in support of these positive effects use standard efficiency explanations from economic theory that broadly fall into two categories: (1) those based on the better matching of pupil needs and school provision; and (2) those based on market discipline incentives. The first argument suggests that gains arise through the efficient allocation of pupils to schools according to personal tastes and pedagogic needs. If schools are allowed some autonomy to differentiate, then pupils can choose the education-service provider that better caters for their needs. This more efficient 'matching' of pupils and schools will lead to higher academic achievements. The second argument is based on competition among schools and market-type incentives. If parents are given freedom to choose the school they prefer, good schools will attract more students and will expand, whereas bad schools will lose pupils and eventually close. In order to remain in the market and keep up with their competitors, schools will have to monitor and improve teaching practices, thus raising educational attainments.

Notice that some important assumptions underlie this model of school provision. First, that schools are able to signal their overall quality to parents via information provided in performance tables, and this drives enrolment patterns. Second, that resources follow pupils – so that pupils are valuable 'assets' for schools – and funding is linked to schools' capacity to attract students. Third, that schools are granted some flexibility to experiment with different teaching methods and to specialise so that they can cater for specific needs or tastes. Schools should also be given some autonomy to manage their teaching body in ways that improve performance and motivation, and to use personnel practices that facilitate the hiring and retaining of talented instructors and managers. Finally, good schools should be allowed to expand in order to accommodate extra demand for their services, and new schools should be allowed in the market if there is demand for their activities. On the other hand, underperforming schools should be allowed to fail and close.

Although models of school provision centred on autonomous structures and choice could deliver improvements in standards, a number of drawbacks have been highlighted. For example, schools could respond to an increase in competition by reducing their teaching effort and going 'down-market' in order to serve only parents with weak preferences for school quality. Moreover, pupils might travel greater distances to attend the school of their choice with consequent detrimental effects on achievement because of lateness, fatigue or absence.

However, the most overarching concerns relate to distributional issues. First of all, although wider school choice could boost some pupils' achievements, these benefits may come at the cost of increased between-school segregation and the gains may not be equally distributed, i.e. school autonomy and choice might not be a 'tide to lift all boats'. The argument behind this claim is twofold. On the one hand, better-off parents might be more effective at exploiting school choice – e.g. because of awareness of educational opportunities and familiarity with the education system – and gain access to high-quality education, while segregating students with the most disadvantaged backgrounds into 'sink-schools'. On the other hand, when standardised exams (feeding into league tables) are high-stakes because they determine reputation and student roll, schools have incentives to cherry-pick students with the 'right' background (a practice called 'cream-skimming').

A related worry is that – even if schools admit disadvantaged pupils – they might try to 'game' or 'twist' the system. For example, teachers might coach only the students most likely to perform well in standardised tests and neglect pupils at the bottom of the ability distribution in order to maximise school ratings. Similarly, schools might exempt more poor-performing students from sitting exams when facing short-run incentives to improve performance, or place more students from low socio-economic backgrounds into special education needs to mitigate their adverse impact on the league tables. Finally, it has been argued that autonomy coupled with account-ability based on league tables might push teachers to train students only to perform well in standardised tests, a problem often referred to as teaching-to-the-test. It is, however, worth noting that the theo-retical considerations in Lazear (2006) suggest that teaching-to-the-test might be more 'efficient' – i.e. produce more learning – when there are disproportionately many high-cost learners in the class. In this sense, predictable high-stakes tests which can be drilled by the teachers might favour students in the tail, who would otherwise leave school even without this basic level of learning.

## School structures in the English system and academies in context

Secondary schools in the state sector in England fall into a number of categories that differ in terms of their governance, management of the teaching staff and control over pupil admissions. Currently, secondary schools can take one of the following six alternative structures: com-munity schools, voluntary controlled schools, foundation schools, voluntary aided schools, city technology colleges, and – since their introduction in the early 2000s – academy schools. In the following paragraphs, we briefly discuss how these school types are structured and highlight their autonomy – or lack of it – in terms of governance and admissions. This will set the ground for a discussion of school academies, which enjoy the most autonomous structures within the state-school system.[3]

Starting with community schools, these institutions are mainly organised and managed through the local authority (LA) and their governing body is predominantly made up of members of staff and representatives of the LA. Responsibility for recruiting, human resources decisions and admissions is in the hands of the LA. As a result, these schools are characterised by very little autonomy and tend to admit local students or students assigned to the school by the LA if they cannot be accommodated in the school of their choice.[4] Next, voluntary controlled schools are similar to community schools in that admissions and employment decisions rest solidly in the hands of the LA. However, most of these schools are religiously denominated and associated with one of the main faiths (mainly Church of England), so their governing body also includes members of the foundation supporting the school.

Voluntary-aided and foundation schools enjoy more autonomy than voluntary controlled and community schools and are similarly structured, except that foundation schools are predominantly secular whereas voluntary aided schools are mainly religiously denominated (Catholic and Church of England). These schools are run as a partnership between the state and the voluntary sector, and the foundation (or the governing body of the school) is responsible for hiring and firing decisions, personnel management and admissions. Note also that the governing body of these schools has a smaller proportion of members of the LA and a significant representation of members of the foundation. In voluntary aided schools, at least half the members are appointed by the foundation.

Like these schools, city technology colleges (CTCs) also enjoy substantial autonomy from the LA. In particular, the majority of their governing body are representatives of the sponsor (usually a business, faith or voluntary group), the school acts as its own admission authority, and the governing body has substantial control over staffing decisions. However, CTCs follow the national curriculum and are characterised by a strong emphasis on technological, scientific and practical subjects.

Lastly, academy schools enjoy a larger degree of autonomy than any other school type in the state system. Academies were gradually introduced into the English school system by the Labour government from September 2002. There are differences in the nature of their introduction in different LAs, but the main aim of the Labour policy was to replace existing failing local schools through conversion to academies.[5] Although academies remain part of the state sector and are non-selective, non-fee-charging state-funded schools, they broadly fall outside the control of the LA in terms of key strategic decisions and day-to-day management. In fact, academies are managed by a private, independent sponsor through a largely self-appointed board of governors. This body has responsibility for hiring the staff, negotiating pay and working conditions, and deciding on matters such as career development, discipline and performance management. Furthermore, some academies (depending on their funding arrangements) enjoy more autonomy in terms of the majority of the taught curriculum (except for English, maths, science and IT), as well as of the structure and length of the school day. Finally, these schools can select up to 10% of their pupils with a clear aptitude in the academy's chosen specialism.

Note that with the election of the Coalition government in 2010, the nature of academies has altered. Many of the new converter academies are not the kinds of disadvantaged institutions that were typical of the Labour-sponsored academies model. As only two years have passed since the Academies Bill 2010 changed the nature of academy schools (and newly introduced free schools), we will not discuss the experience and likely effects of the new wave of academies.[6] We confine our attention to the Labour academies, i.e. those introduced up to the academic year 2008/9, when there were 130 academies operating, comprising approximately 4.5% of secondary schools.[7]

## School structures and school autonomy: evidence from England

We will now discuss the evidence from England on the effects of school structure and autonomy on both pupils' performance and school intake. When thinking about the impact of school autonomy, the most pertinent example is the one of academy schools. However, at present, very limited evidence has been collected on this relatively recent 'policy experiment'. Therefore, we begin by reviewing some closely related topics, namely the effects of accountability, other forms of school autonomy and choice in the 'education market'.

A broad literature has investigated the effects of the education reforms of the late 1980s which led to the publication of performance tables in 1992 and the introduction of parental choice as the guiding principle for pupils' assignment to schools (see Glennerster, 1991). For example, Levacic (2004) reports that secondary school head teachers respond to competitive pressures due to the introduction of performance tables, and Bradley et al. (2000) show that secondary schools that performed better than their neighbours attracted more pupils. More recently, Burgess et al. (2010) study the abolition of performance tables in Wales and find that reducing accountability significantly worsens school effectiveness.

One very illustrative example based on the reforming experience of the late 1980s is Clark (2009). The author investigates whether secondary schools that were handed more autonomy following conversion to grant-maintained (GM) status (roughly corresponding to foundation schools today) performed better than schools that did not convert. More specifically, the author examines the fact that parents with children enrolled at the school had to vote on the decision to become GM, and compares the performance of 'narrow winners' with 'narrow losers' to identify the effects of autonomous structures. Clark finds that becoming a GM school is associated with significant improvements in the proportion of pupils achieving five or more GCSEs at A*–C grades (or equivalent). Moreover, this advantage increases over time, with schools improving at an increasing rate after conversion to their more autonomous structure. Student 'quality' (i.e. pupil intake) also improves in schools converting to GM status, suggesting that they might become more selective, or that parental preferences for these schools might change upon conversion. On the other hand, the author does not investigate whether the effects of more autonomy are heterogeneous according to students' background, so that it is hard to say whether GM status improved learning of students in the tail.

In a related piece, Gibbons and Silva (2011) study the effect of attending an autonomous school – i.e. a voluntary aided or a foundation school – during primary education for more recent years (i.e. mid-2000s). Their approach exploits access to information about pupils' place of residence, previous academic records and future (secondary) school choice to control for factors that influence the propensity to attend an autonomous school. The authors' results suggest that although more autonomous schools tend to admit pupils with educationally advantageous backgrounds, there are no clear performance benefits from autonomous structures. This is true irrespective of pupils' background: students eligible for free school meals, carrying special education needs and with low early test scores (age 7/Key Stage 1 achievements) in more autonomous schools finish primary education neither better nor worse than comparable students in LA-controlled community schools. However, Gibbons et al. (2008) find that primary schools with autonomous governance respond to a greater degree of competition with other local schools by raising their pupils' achievements: their students' Key Stage 1-to-Key Stage 2 value-added improves by about 1.6 points for each additional competitor, or about 16–19 weeks of progress in one of the core subjects, i.e. English or mathematics. The authors also find that this effect is somewhat larger for pupils from a disadvantaged background – i.e. those eligible for free school meals – although the data are 'thin' and inference less precise. This suggests that pupils in the tail might benefit from studying at more autonomous schools when these have to compete with other local institutions. On the other hand, the authors find no evidence that increased school competition improves standards for pupils in schools that fall more heavily under the control of the LA (e.g. community schools). These patterns lend some support to the idea that increased parental choice can lead to an improvement in standards in education when coupled with a sufficient degree of school autonomy. Consistent results are also documented in Gibbons and Silva (2008), who investigate the effectiveness of secondary schools in more dense urban environments, where the most disadvantaged students – i.e. those in the tail – tend to live. The authors show that students attending more urban secondary schools perform better than those enrolled at more isolated rural institutions, and suggest that a likely explanation of their findings lies in greater school choice and competition in denser urban environments.

As discussed above, the main concern with increased school autonomy and choice is that these arrangements might trigger perverse school behaviour and, in particular, efforts to 'game the system' and 'cream-skim' the best students. Evidence on the first issue is fairly scant, even though Burgess et al. (2005) show results consistent with the idea that accountability and autonomy have diverted teachers' attention away from low-ability pupils towards students most likely to achieve high marks and improve school rankings. In contrast, more research effort has been directed at understanding the effects of choice and autonomy on segregation. Among others, Bradley et al. (2000), Bradley and Taylor (2002), Goldstein and Noden (2003), and Burgess et al. (2004) all suggest that increased parental choice and differentiated school markets (i.e. different schools with different structures) are associated with more polarisation in secondary schools. Gibbons and Silva (2006) analyse this issue at the primary school level and find that more school choice tends to exacerbate polarisation of primary schools by student attainment, although this effect is not statistically significant. On the other hand, Gorard et al. (2003) show that secondary schools became less socially segregated in the 1990s after the introduction of the market-oriented reforms during the late 1980s, and Burgess et al. (2010) find no evidence of reduced sorting in Welsh schools after the abolition of performance tables in 2001.

Direct evidence on the effect of autonomous structures as embodied by the academy schools is much more limited. Two early studies were conducted by Machin and Wilson (2008) and PriceWaterhouse-Coopers (2008). The former looked at possible improvements in the GCSE performance of academy schools relative to the achievement of a matched group of schools, and found modest and insignificant effects. Conversely, the latter compared the evolution of achievements in academies with the attainment in the national average, and found large and significant effects. However, as Machin and Wilson (2008) argue, comparing achievements at academies with the average national performance is very problematic and the results by Price-WaterhouseCoopers should be interpreted with caution. Interestingly, the two studies agree that – back in 2008 – it might have been too early to draw conclusions on the general effectiveness of academies. More recent evidence collected in Machin and Vernoit (2011) presents a rosier picture: the authors show that moving to a more autonomous school structure by converting to an academy generates improvement in terms of pupils' performance at the end of secondary school. Importantly, the authors find that these results are stronger for academies that experienced the largest increase in their school autonomy (i.e. from community schools to academies) and only significant and sizeable for academies that opened earlier on (i.e. up to the academic year 2006–7). These early reformers experience improvements in the fraction of pupils obtaining five or more A*–C GCSEs of around 18% of a standard deviation, or approximately 3.5 percentage points from an average of 30%.

Machin and Vernoit (2011) and Wilson (2011) study changes in the pupil intake composition of schools becoming academies. Both studies find that the Key Stage 2 scores of Year 7 pupils entering academies significantly improved after conversion. Further, both papers document that this improvement occurred in 'one shot' as schools changed their status and that the jump was sizeable at approximately 1.5–3% improvement in average Key Stage 2 achievements. Wilson (2011) further documents that this average improvement was accompanied by a significant reduction of the standard deviation of the Key Stage 2 scores of the incoming cohorts of Year 7 pupils at converting academies, implying that overall these schools reduced their intake of pupils from the lower tail of the ability distribution. Finally, the author documents that converting academies enrolled approximately 12.5% fewer pupils who are eligible for free school meals, reinforcing the impression that academies became more 'exclusive'. However, lacking information on parental preferences, neither study can tell apart whether changes occurred because of school admissions practices or changes in parental preferences for this type of more autonomous school.

One thing remarkably absent from these studies on the effects of academies is an investigation of whether any improvements in school performance occurred by 'lifting' pupils in the tail or by further pushing up students at the top of the ability distribution. Using the same data and approach as Machin and Vernoit (2011), we next turn to this question. In a nutshell, we investigate the Key Stage 4 (GCSE) performance effects of academy conversion across the distribution of pupil prior attainment, whereas Machin and Vernoit (2011) looked only at average effects. For comparison, they found an average improvement of 0.148 of a standard deviation in the fraction of pupils obtaining five or more A\*–C GCSEs for early academy conversions, but could not reject a zero impact for later conversions.

Figure 7.1 on page 108 summarises the findings from our new analysis, while the actual results from our statistical regression approach are presented in Table 7.1 on page 109. In the top plot, pupils are ranked by their Key Stage 2 total score (percentile) within their secondary school (e.g. the bottom 10% at the school), whereas in the bottom plot they are ranked within the national distribution (e.g. the bottom 10% nationwide).[8] This alternative ranking allows us to account for the possibility that pupils in the middle of the ability distribution at an academy school might still be in the tail nationwide since academies enrol the most disadvantaged students. Our findings reveal that the positive average effect of early converters documented by Machin and Vernoit (2011) and reported in the first pair of bars arises from significant effects higher up the distribution of students' early test scores. There are positive, statistically significant effects (represented by a full bar in the plots) in the 50th-to-80th and top 20 percentiles of the within-school distribution. Similarly, there are positive and sizeable effects in the 25th-to-50th and top 20 percentiles in the national distribution, and very large positive effects for pupils in the 50th-to-80th percentile of the national distribution. Although these effects are not significant, they are clearly much larger than those for pupils at the bottom of the ability distribution. Indeed, irrespective of whether we rank pupils by the school or national ability distribution, the effects of academy conversion are insignificantly different from zero – and possibly negative for later conversions – in the bottom 10% and 20% of the ability distribution, suggesting no beneficial effects on tail students in academies.

## What do we learn from other countries' experiences? The case of the USA and Sweden

England is not the only country where reforms aimed at giving schools more autonomy and freedom to innovate have taken place. In the USA, charter schools – a type of institution similar to academies, with significant autonomy in terms of management and decision-making – have spread across many states since their introduction in the 1990s. Similarly, a reform implemented in Sweden in 1992 brought to the 'education market' free schools – i.e. private schools competing with public institutions for students and public funding, but privately managed and with significant autonomy in terms of their day-to-day activities and long-term choices. Since we believe these experiences provide some useful lessons for the 'academies experiment' in the UK, we briefly review some related evidence.

Starting with the USA, a number of studies have obtained causal estimates of the effect of charter schools by exploiting the fact that oversubscribed institutions use lotteries to allocate places, therefore bypassing the problem of selection of different pupils into charter schools.[9] One of the earliest studies, by Abdulkadiroglu et al. (2009), focuses on the impact of the Boston charter schools on pupil attainments. The authors find significant improvement in pupils' test scores both in middle and high schools, and for both English and mathematics. Interestingly, the authors also show that pupils previously in the tail benefit the most. Similarly, Hoxby and Murarka (2009) find positive and significant effects of charter school attendance for students 'lotteried in' to the New York City charter schools. For both reading and mathematics, these beneficial effects increase for each additional year spent at a charter school between 3rd and 8th grade. These effects are remarkably similar for boys and girls, and for students of Black and Hispanic origin, suggesting that students in the tail might benefit from charter school attendance. A related study by Dobbie and Fryer (2009) investigates the educational attainments of children enrolled at charter schools associated with the Harlem Children's Zone (HCZ) initiative in New York. Attendance at an HCZ school significantly increases pupils' achievement, with sizeable improvements in English and mathematics for both primary and secondary school students. The programme benefits pupils of all abilities, who attained roughly similar benefits from attending HCZ charters. Finally, Angrist et al. (2010) evaluate the impact of a group of charter schools in Lynn (Massachusetts) managed by the Knowledge is Power Program (KIPP). These charter institutions specifically aim at improving achievements of low-income students who qualify for free school meals and were set up by teachers qualified through the Teach for America programme. Pupils enrolled at KIPP schools between grades five and eight experience sizeable improvements in their English and mathematics achievements. Importantly, these benefits are particularly strong for pupils with special education needs, lower prior attainments and poor command of English. Stated differently, the benefits of attending a KIPP school are stronger for pupils in the tail.

It should be noted that none of these studies can properly investigate whether charter schools have more selected intake composition, since the allocation of places at over-subscribed schools is done by lotteries. However, most of these charter schools tend to cater to very disadvantaged (and mainly ethnic-minority) urban students and thus predominantly enrol students in the bottom tail of the achievement distribution. For example, Hoxby and Murarka (2009) report that the New York City schools they analyse are in very deprived areas and attract students who are substantially poorer than those at an average public school in New York City.

Regarding the Swedish experience, a number of studies have investigated the competition effects exerted by the introduction of independent free schools either on state school performance or on aggregate achievements at the municipality level. These studies include Ahlin (2003), Björklund et al. (2005), and Sandström and Bergström (2005), with results ranging from statistically insignificant estimates to very large effects. However, the early version of the work by Böhlmark and Lindahl (2007) is the only study that carefully decomposes whether any improvement in attainments at the municipal level can be explained by state schools responding to the free school competitive threat by raising standards, or by free schools being more effective and expanding their market shares. The authors show that the former channel explains most of the improvements in overall achievements, but also provide some evidence that free schools – with their more autonomous structures – are more effective at educating children. Note that this effect is small – especially compared with the results found for the US charter schools – at approximately I percentile or 4% of a standard deviation, and that Böhlmark and Lindahl (2007) do not report whether these results are stronger for weaker pupils with a more disadvantaged background. Finally, the authors investigate whether the increased availability of private schools in the municipality has worsened school-level segregation along the lines of parental income, education and immigration status. Their results show that more private schools tend to 'siphon away' from public schools children whose parents have higher education levels and who are not first-generation immigrants. This suggests that Swedish free schools tend to enrol pupils not coming from the bottom tail of the ability distribution.


## Concluding remarks

The notion that different school structures can be a route to deliver improved educational performance has become popular. Indeed, reforms to school structures – and their autonomy and governance – have been a feature of recent education policies in countries like England, Sweden and the United States. But does autonomy offer scope to improve the lot of disadvantaged students in the lower tail of the education distribution?

Our conclusion is probably not, or at least not in England and in the case of Labour's sponsored academies. On balance, the evidence available shows at best only small beneficial effects on overall pupil performance and very little consistent evidence of improvements for tail students. Nevertheless, there are some success stories coming from the USA, suggesting that, in some situations, autonomous schools can improve the performance of disadvantaged students, and narrow some of the most persistent educational disparities, such as the black–white achievement gap.

What could explain the different performance of the US charters and UK academies? Although very speculative, one possible explanation rests with the details of the functioning of American charter schools. One of the defining features of these institutions is that they operate on the basis of a 'charter', i.e. a performance contract granted for three to five years, defining the school's mission and goals, as well as the type of students it aims to attract. Charter schools are then held accountable to their sponsor (for example a local school board), which assesses whether these stated aims have been achieved and – if not – eventually revokes the charter. As of 2012, approximately 15% of all charter schools had closed because they failed to achieve their goals. This generates sharp incentives for these schools to 'perform' and achieve their contractual aims. Since the majority of charter schools serve impoverished urban areas with the specific aim of improving the attainment of disadvantaged pupils – and are held accountable for their improvements – it is not surprising that these institutions have been effective at educating the 'tail'.

On the other hand, English academies cater for a mix of students of different abilities, and are held accountable on the basis of the same performance tables used by other schools in the country. These tend to focus schools' attention on final attainments – such as the proportion of students achieving five A*–C GCSEs – rather than measures of educational progression – such as contextual value-added. As discussed above and elsewhere in this book (see Chapter 12), this has the potential to distort schools' incentives towards coaching students most likely to perform well in the national exams in order to maximise school ratings, and neglect pupils at the bottom of the ability distribution. Unfortunately, the evidence we have collected seems to back this pessimistic intuition.

In conclusion, it may be that in the longer run the best academies will flourish and spread their practices across the education market in a tide that lifts all boats and so raises the achievement of pupils of all abilities. However, in order to guarantee that these more autonomous institutions can make a difference for the tail, new 'rules of the game' should be designed to make sure that schools have incentives to focus on the most disadvantaged students and, at the same time, are held accountable for their improvements.

## References

Abdulkadiroglu, A., J. Angrist, S. Dynarski, T. Kane and P. Pathak (2009) 'Accountability and Flexibility in Public Schools:

Evidence from Boston's Charters and Pilots', NBER Working Paper 15549.

Ahlin, Å (2003) 'Does School Competition Matter? Effects of a Large-scale School Choice Reform on Student Performance', Working Paper 2003:2, Department of Economics, Uppsala University.

Angrist, J., S. Dynarski, T. Kane, P. Pathak and C. Walters (2010) 'Who Benefits from Charter Schools? Evidence from KIPP Lynn', NBER Working Paper 15740.

Björklund, A., M. Clark, P.-A. Edin, P. Fredriksson and A. Krueger (2005) 'The Market Comes to Education in Sweden: An Evaluation of Sweden's Surprising School Reforms', New York, Russell Sage Foundation.

Böhlmark, A. and M. Lindahl (2007) 'The Impact of School Choice on Pupil Achievement, Segregation and Costs: Swedish Evidence', IZA Discussion Paper No. 2786.

Bradley, S., R. Crouchley, J. Millington and J. Taylor (2000) 'Testing for Quasi-Market Forces in Secondary Education', *Oxford Bulletin of Economics and Statistics*, vol. 62(3), pp. 357–390.

Bradley, S. and J. Taylor (2002) 'The Effect of the Quasi-Market on the Efficiency-Equity Trade-off in the Secondary School Sector', *Bulletin of Economic Research*, vol. 54, pp. 295–314.

Burgess, S., A. Briggs, B. McConnell and H. Slater (2006) 'School Choice in England: Background Facts', CMPO Working Paper 06/159.

Burgess, S., B. McConnell, C. Propper and D. Wilson (2004) 'Sorting and Choice in English Secondary Schools', CMPO Working Paper 04/111.

Burgess, S., C. Propper, H. Slater and D. Wilson (2005) 'Who Wins and Who Loses from School Accountability? The Distribution of Educational Gains in English Secondary Schools', CMPO Working Paper 05/128.

Burgess, S., D. Wilson and J. Worth (2010) 'A Natural Experiment in School Accountability: The Impact of School Performance Information on Pupil Progress and Sorting', CMPO Working Paper 10/246.

Clark, D. (2009) 'Politics, Markets and Schools: Quasi-Experimental Estimates of the Impact of Autonomy and Competition from a Truly Revolutionary UK Reform', *Journal of Political Economy*, vol. 117(4), pp. 745–783.

CREDO (2009) 'Multiple Choice: Charter Performance in Sixteen States', Center for Research on Education Outcomes, Stanford University.

Dobbie, W. and R. Fryer (2009) 'Are High Quality Schools Enough to Close the Achievement Gap? Evidence from a Social Experiment in Harlem', NBER Working Paper 15473.

Gibbons, S., S. Machin and O. Silva (2008) 'Choice, Competition and Pupil Achievement', *Journal of the European Economic Association*, vol. 6(4), pp. 912–947.

Gibbons, S. and O. Silva (2006) 'Competition and Accessibility in School Markets: Empirical Analysis using Boundary Discontinuities', in T.J. Gronberg and D.W. Jansen (eds), 'Improving School Accountability: Check-Ups or Choice?', *Advances in Applied Microeconomics*, vol. 14, Elsevier.

Gibbons, S. and O. Silva (2008) 'Urban Density and Pupil Achievement', *Journal of Urban Economics*, vol. 63(1), pp. 631–650.

Gibbons, S. and O. Silva (2011) 'Faith Primary Schools: Better Schools or Better Pupils?', *Journal of Labor Economics*, vol. 29(3), pp. 589–635.

Glennerster, H. (1991) 'Quasi-Markets for Education', *Economic Journal*, vol. 101, pp. 1268–1276.

Goldstein, H. and P. Noden (2003) 'Modelling Social Segregation', *Oxford Review of Education*, vol. 29(2), pp. 225–237.

Gorard, S., C. Taylor and J. Fitz (2003) *Schools, Markets and Choice Policies*, London, Routledge Farmer.

Hanushek, E. (2003) 'The Failure of Input-Based Policies', *Economic Journal*, vol. 113, F64–F98.

Hoxby, C. (2004) 'School Choice and School Competition: Evidence from the United States', *Swedish Economic Policy Review*, vol. 10(2), pp. 9–65.

Hoxby, C. and S. Murarka (2007) 'Methods of Assessing Achievement of Students in Charter Schools', in M. Behrens (ed.), *Charter School Outcomes*, New York, The Analytic Press.

Hoxby, C. and S. Murarka (2009) 'Charter Schools in New York City: Who Enrolls and How They Affect Student Achievement', NBER Working Paper 14852.

Lazear, E. (2006) 'Speeding, Tax Fraud and Teaching to the Test', *Quarterly Journal of Economics*, vol. 121(3), pp. 1029–1061.

Le Grand, J. (1991) *Equity and Choice*, London, Harper Collins.

Le Grand, J. (1993) *Quasi-Markets and Social Policy*, London, Macmillan.

Levacic, R. (2004) 'Competition and the Performance of English Secondary Schools: Further Evidence', *Education Economics*, vol. 12(2), pp. 177–193.

Machin, S. and J. Vernoit (2011) 'Changing School Autonomy: Academy Schools and Their Introduction to England's Education', CEE Discussion Paper 123.

Machin, S. and A. Vignoles (2005) *What's the Good of Education?*, Princeton, Princeton University Press.

Machin, S. and J. Wilson (2008) 'Public and Private Schooling Initiatives in England: The Case of City Academies', in R. Chakrabarti and P. Peterson (eds), *School Choice International*, Cambridge, MA, MIT Press.

PriceWaterhouseCoopers (2008) 'Academies Evaluation Fifth Annual Report', Annesley, Department for Children, School and Families (DCSF) Publications.

Sandström, M. and Bergström, F. (2005) 'School Vouchers in Practice: Competition Will Not Hurt You', *Journal of Public Economics*, vol. 89, pp. 351–380.

Tiebout, C. (1956) 'A Pure Theory of Local Expenditures', *Journal of Political Economy*, vol. 64(5), pp. 416–424.

Wilson, J. (2011) 'Are England's Academies More Inclusive or More "Exclusive"? The Impact of Institutional Change on the Pupil Profile of Schools', CEE Discussion Paper 125.

Figure 7.1 **Academies and GCSE performance – the effect of academy conversion on pupils of different abilities**

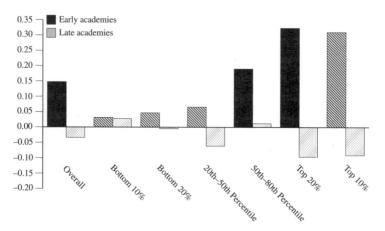

*Pupils ranked by percentile within school distribution*

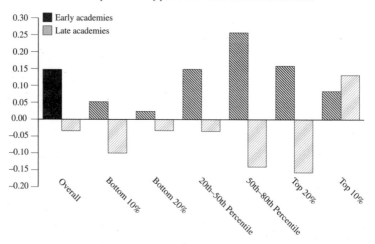

*Pupils ranked by percentile within national distribution*

Note: The outcome of interest is the fraction of pupils obtaining at least five A*–C GCSE, and the bars show the effect of early and late academy conversions expressed as a fraction of the across-school variation (standard deviation) in the percentage of pupils achieving five A*–C GCSE. Pupils are ranked by their KS2 total score within their secondary school in the top panel (e.g. the bottom 10% at the school) and in the national distribution in the bottom panel (e.g. the bottom 10% nation-wide). For details about the regression method and specification see notes to Table 7.1. Early academies are those converting before 2006/2007. Full bar represents significant effects (10% significance or better), shaded bars represent non-significant effects.

**Table 7.1: Academies and GCSE performance – the effect of academy conversion on pupils of different abilities**

| Pupil KS2 between: | Bottom 10 pctiles | Bottom 20 pctiles | 20th–50th pctile | 50th–80th pctile | Top 20 pctiles | Top 10 pctiles |
|---|---|---|---|---|---|---|
| *Panel A: Pupils ranked by percentile within school distribution* | | | | | | |
| Early Academies, | 0.032 | 0.047 | 0.066 | 0.190 | 0.323 | 0.310 |
| Stand. Effect | (0.076) | (0.072) | (0.048) | (0.091)* | (0.175)* | (0.228) |
| Late Academies, | 0.028 | –0.005 | –0.061 | 0.012 | –0.096 | –0.091 |
| Stand. Effect | (0.039) | (0.037) | (0.057) | (0.086) | (0.142) | (0.166) |
| *Panel B: Pupils ranked by percentile within national distribution* | | | | | | |
| Early Academies, | 0.052 | 0.024 | 0.149 | 0.257 | 0.159 | 0.084 |
| Stand. Effect | (0.135) | (0.082) | (0.102) | (0.161) | (0.274) | (0.280) |
| Late Academies, | –0.100 | –0.033 | –0.035 | –0.140 | –0.157 | 0.132 |
| Stand. Effect | (0.061) | (0.052) | (0.089) | (0.142) | (0.233) | (0.197) |

Note: The dependent variable is the fraction of pupils obtaining at least five A\*–C GCSE grades. Pupils are ranked by their KS2 total score within their secondary school in Panel A (e.g. the bottom 10% at the school) and in the national distribution in Panel B (e.g. the bottom 10% nationwide). Regressions include school fixed effects, year dummies, KS2 of pupils taking their KS4 exams and the following controls: proportion of pupils eligible for free school meals; proportion of pupils taking free school meals; proportion of pupils of White ethnic origin; pupil to qualified teachers ratio; proportion of pupils with special education needs, with statements; proportion of pupils with special education needs, without statements. Number of observations: 1560. Early academies are those converting before 2006/2007. Standard errors in parenthesis clustered at the school level. \*=10% significance or better.

# 8

# What does good upper secondary education for the tail – and maybe everyone – look like?

*Tina Isaacs*

As Chris Husbands deftly argues in Chapter 10, 'it's the teachers, stupid' (with apologies to Bill Clinton). Good teachers are passionate and knowledgeable about their subjects and can inspire the children they teach to achieve what we might have thought them incapable of. Excellent teachers are a necessary, but not sufficient, factor in trying to solve the education problems of the bottom quintile of students. What those students learn matters as well. This essay argues against the received wisdom in the UK, which is that lower achievers should focus on vocational qualifications and be taught in a different way from other students. Instead, I will argue that, just as much as anyone else, lower achievers deserve a good general education, and that we should look not solely to vocational options as the solution to the low achievement/disengagement of some 14- to 16-year-olds, nor relegate 16- to 18-year-olds to a purely vocational diet if they do not achieve five or more A*–C grade GCSEs (or their EBC equivalents). I also argue that, if we shift our focus away from qualification achievement and concentrate more on what we believe to be a good curricular offer for secondary students we could allow some of them – both in the tail and also in the other group (almost 30%)

who fail to achieve the requisite qualifications at 16 – the opportunity to do so by 17 or 18.

## Background

As earlier essays in this book have pointed out, much of the achievement gap between the highest- and lowest-achieving students at age 16 has been there since primary school or even before (Clifton and Cook, 2012). So unfortunately there is only so much that can be done to narrow the gap once students embark on upper secondary programmes (which I define here as Year 10 and above). But we should try to avoid expanding the gap, or thinking that it is the inevitable product of some young people being 'academic' (our children) or 'non-academic' (other people's children). The challenge we face is a big one. A recent (2010) study by the National Research and Development Centre for Adult Literacy and Numeracy (NRDC) has shown that the literacy and numeracy proficiency of 16- to 19-year-olds has been relatively stable over the past 20 years or so, with about 22% functionally innumerate and 17% functionally illiterate (Rashid and Brooks, 2010), numbers that uncannily parallel what we are calling 'the tail'. If you're innumerate, you have only the most basic skills in computation and mathematical comprehension, which means you cannot deal with most of the mathematical challenges that life throws at you. England's 2009 PISA results showed that almost 20% of 15-year-olds functioned below level 2 in mathematical literacy, again a number that corresponds with 'the tail'. If you're functionally illiterate, you can only read simple texts and answer straightforward questions on them (as long as you're not distracted by other information). The ability to make inferences and understand indirect meaning is very limited, which again means that full participation in work, family and civic life is difficult (Rashid and Brooks, 2010). And the PISA 2009 reading scores from England confirm this bleak picture – 18% scored below level 2, which PISA characterises as basic literacy. Of the countries with which we constantly compare ourselves, Singapore has only 12.4% below level 2, Finland only 8.1% (OECD 2010).

So there's a pretty clear rationale for prioritising English/literacy and mathematics/numeracy[1] for older children as much as for younger ones. And almost everyone engaged in writing about good curriculum provision for 14- to 16-year-olds seems to agree on this point. After that, however, consensus breaks down.

## Curriculum focus rather than qualifications

One of the issues about the debate around good secondary provision is its starting point – with qualifications, not the content of the curriculum itself. England's practice of providing separate subject qualifications – the outcome of a course of study leading to a certificate of accomplishment in a particular area – is unusual. Much more commonly a country or a region recognises the end of upper secondary education through an inclusive school leaving certificate or diploma, which includes attainment records on more than one subject area and can be used for entrance to higher education or employment, for example the US high school diploma or the French baccalaureate. Almost no country, aside from some former British colonies, has an examination system for both 16- and 18-year-olds like our GCSEs and A levels. Aside from shifting the emphasis from what students should know and be able to do to how many examinations they can pass, the advent of subject-based qualifications has allowed the government to measure success in upper secondary education by the number of qualifications 14- to 18-year-olds achieve and how well they do in them. This has led to ever-increasing government regulation and involvement, and the concomitant withdrawal of autonomy and independence for schools over what to teach and how to teach it.

Because we have qualifications for separate subjects, and because schools are accountable for their students' performance on those qualifications, the notion of a broad and balanced education – to use a hackneyed phrase – gets short shrift. To my mind a 14 to 16 education worth having includes that which produces students who can progress to further education comfortably, but that also provides them with the grounding they need to thrive in later life: English, mathematics and science, obviously, but also the cultural capital that history in its broadest sense, which includes geographical, political, economic and social/cultural perspectives, and modern languages provide. However, schools, because they have every incentive to do so, enter students onto qualifications that will provide the highest payback in terms of grades. They also concentrate on those students who are most likely to achieve good grades, and especially on those on the cusp of achieving good grades, at the expense of those who are more likely to get Es, Fs and Gs in their GCSEs. This means that two insidious forces are at work simultaneously – what you learn doesn't really matter as long as you get C or better on it, and you get taught by the 'best' teachers only if your qualification results are likely to redound to the credit of your school.

A curriculum-based system, on the other hand, is predicated on the notion that there is a worthwhile set of knowledge, skills and understandings that *all* students should have access to, regardless of the outcomes. It should have both the depth and breadth to prepare students to progress to further and/or higher education, for work, for family life and for social and civic participation. The original national curriculum for 14- to 16-year-olds incorporated this notion, even if it was linked to the qualifications that took over from O levels and CSEs, the GCSEs. It required students to take a modern foreign language, technology, history, geography, art, music and physical education, as well as the 'core' of English, mathematics and science. While we might question whether those same subjects would be the ones we'd want to include in a curriculum in 2013 as opposed to 1988, its underpinning assumption was that this was a curriculum for all. That curriculum was never fully implemented, and the 1993 Dearing Report, *The National Curriculum and Its Assessment*, recommended that art, geography, history and music become optional subjects. It broke down further, I believe, because of the inextricable link to time-limited qualifications and to the accountability regime that was put into place once Labour came into power in 1997. First, schools were allowed to 'disapply' certain subjects – modern foreign languages, design and technology, science – for certain students. Then in 2004 languages and design and technology became completely optional and participation in them dropped precipitously. The advent of the so-called English baccalaureate (EBacc), and the more recent announcement that English Baccalaureate Certificates (EBCs) will replace GCSEs, does not herald the return to a curriculum-based view of schooling because it, too, is an accountability measure of sorts, even if it claims to be simply a performance measure. It widens the subjects reported each year to include science, languages and either history or geography, but it is based on achievement of grade C or above on five rather than two subjects and therefore creates no incentive for schools to make this a curriculum for all or to encourage students in the tail to take them. The EBacc certainly has had an effect, but on higher achievers rather than anyone else. The simple fact of the government publishing how many students achieved A*–C grades in all five subjects caused schools to increase the number of their students taking those subjects from 22% in 2010 to 49% in 2014 (DfE, 2012). It's no surprise that the last number mirrors the approximate numbers schools expect are capable of achieving high grades.

For lower achievers the Labour government promoted a programme called Foundation Learning, once again revolving around qualifications achievement, this time at Entry Level (national curriculum levels 1 to 4) and Level 1 (GCSE grades G to D). Because the qualifications needed to be on the Qualifications and Credit Framework (QCF), they did not include GCSEs themselves, which are outside the framework. The programme's aim was to increase 'engagement, participation and progression ... toward Level 2 [qualifications]' through qualifications in subjects or vocational areas, functional skills and personal and social development (LSIS, no date). In fact, very few Entry and Level 1 stand-alone (as opposed to foundation tier GCSEs) qualifications are subject-based. The vast majority are personal and employment skills based, which leads us to the next conundrum in trying to think through appropriate secondary learning for the tail – whether it should be skills- or subject-based.

## Subjects versus skills

There seems to be a policy consensus in England that lower achievers need a skills-based rather than a subject- or knowledge-based curriculum. As Michael Young persuasively writes, government policy on education until recently systematically marginalised knowledge (Young, 2011). Instead, in the name of learner-centred education, the focus shifted to learning styles, outcomes and employability, all of which are content-free. As seen in the emphases in Foundation Learning, this was especially true for lower achievers. Skills-based learning was somehow seen as more manageable for and relevant to those who did not do particularly well in school and was introduced for laudable reasons; those who promote it believe that skills-based learning is more inclusive and interesting and can capture the imagination of students in a way that knowledge-based learning cannot.

In addition, the changes to the Key Stage 3 curriculum that were put in place for 11- to 14-year-olds in 2007 were based on the premise that the role of education is to create successful learners, confident individuals and responsible citizens – educational aims with which no one would disagree. However, the method for achieving the aims was couched in terms of 'planned learning experiences' that gave priority to 'approaches to learning' and 'cross-curriculum dimensions'. Students were to concentrate on Personal Learning and Thinking Skills (PLTS): independent enquiry; creative thinking; reflective learning; teamwork; self-management; and effective participation alongside functional skills in English, mathematics and ICT. All this was in the name of relevance and supposed student interest. Subject knowledge, while included, seemed to be an afterthought. Before a parallel, skills-based approach could be introduced for Key Stages 1 and 2 in 2011 Labour lost the 2010 election and the Coalition government announced a review of the national curriculum.

Its curriculum model, as Young (2011, p. 4) points out, is deeply traditional, based on fact-gathering and memorisation – 'a curriculum based on compliance' – which probably is not accessible to all learners, rather than what he characterises as a 'curriculum based on engagement' that features content but is based on the understanding of concepts and universal values. Young argues that it is through the emphasis on understanding important concepts, which are not necessarily fixed, through clear subject study, that all students are treated equally 'and not just members of different social classes, different ethnic groups or as boys or girls' (Young 2011, p. 18). He might have added different learning styles and different content to study to the list of things that promote difference, since most people assume that children who belong to the tail need both different teaching and learning methods and a different curriculum, which leads us to our next topic – whether lower achievers should primarily be fed a diet of basic skills plus vocationally related content.

## The general versus vocational debate

Over the course of the last few decades, as the school leaving age was raised first to 15, then to 16 (and it's soon to be 18, although technically the 'participation' age is what is being raised and post-16 a person would only have to be engaged in some education-related activity approximately one day per week), the education system has been freighted with ever-expanding social and economic burdens. Governments associate education with international economic competitiveness and also increasingly expect schools to take on the social burdens of moulding and shaping responsible and law-abiding citizens. For lower achievers, successive governments' answer to both issues has been the proliferation of vocationally related qualifications.[2] These qualifications have myriad (and conflicting) expectations attached to them. They are supposed to motivate the disaffected and those in danger of dropping out, prepare students for the world of work, solve basic literacy and numeracy problems, maintain high standards and 'parity of esteem' with academic qualifications, and lead to success in entry to higher education.

The Labour government, in its belief in the efficacy of vocationally related qualifications, promoted nationally based qualifications such as GNVQs, VCEs, applied GCSEs, applied A levels and the Diploma. It also expanded the qualifications that counted towards achievement and attainment tables to include GCSE 'equivalents' – thousands of them, some of them notionally the size of four GCSEs. A QCA report published in October 2002 stated that there had been overwhelming support to include vocationally related qualifications in performance tables, while recognising that schools would use qualifications to get the most points possible. It went on to state that 'in the majority of cases decisions will be made in students' best interests' (quoted in Wolf, 2010, p. 3). Schools quickly rushed to put students on these courses – the number of Key Stage 4 students enrolled in vocationally related qualifications at Level 2 (GCSE grades A*–C), including BTEC Firsts, expanded from 1,882 in 2003/4 to 462,182 in 2009/10 (Wolf, 2010, p. 47). Schools were clearly seeking to improve their position in performance tables and reduce the possibility of being put into special measures by encouraging or even forcing their students onto vocationally related courses, where they were more likely to get a C grade or above, which would then count for up to four grade Cs. Examination entries for subjects that I believe would increase the likelihood of students gaining full participation in society, such as languages, continued to decrease in number. When Harris and Burn (2011) conducted a survey about the decline in history GCSEs, schools told them that history was competing with subjects that were thought to be easier, or offered more 'value' – value being described as courses that produced the equivalent of four GCSEs, many of which were given the teaching time equivalent of two GCSEs (p. 254). Once down the pathway of having the bulk of studies, aside from those that the national curriculum compels – English, mathematics and science – outside the mainstream it is almost impossible for a student to progress to a more academic route post-16.

Graham and Tyler (quoted in Higham and Yeomans, 2007, p. 288) foresaw the problem in 1992 when they wrote that

> *The other solution [to Key Stage 4 issues] was simply to say that at 14 children could, with certain exceptions, choose what they wanted to study ... this would be turning our backs on the benefits of the national curriculum. A country whose state education service had been bedevilled by patchiness and a lack of entitlement had at last got itself a national curriculum which it should hang on to at all costs ...*

But until the Wolf Review (2010) and its acceptance by the Coalition government changed the course of national provision at Key Stage 4, too many students were pursuing NVQs and/or vocationally related courses worth four GCSEs, not because of curricular considerations, but because achievement on those courses helped their schools' performance table positions. But while the outcomes of Wolf put paid to the worst excesses of over-reliance on vocationally related provision, recommending that no 14- to 16-year-old should spend more than 20% of his or her time on vocationally related qualifications and stating that all qualifications would be counted as just one GCSE for performance table purposes, the policy that followed Wolf was still couched in the language of qualifications accrual and of grades C and above. This is of little help, at present, to the tail of underachievers, who are more likely to be getting five Es than five Cs, and whose educational provision therefore does not play as much into schools' decisions about whether to condemn them to diets of less-respected qualifications.

What the Wolf Review did prove was that schools were placing Key Stage 4 students on vocationally related qualifications 'for reasons which have nothing to do with their own long-term interests, within education or the labour market. They can and do find that they are unable, as a result, to progress to the courses they want and have been led to expect they will enter' (Wolf, 2010, p. 81). Students were aware of the GCSE equivalence of the qualifications they set out to take, but not of the real equivalence, which was considerably less. One assistant college principal told Wolf that

> the incentive for schools to provide qualifications for their pupils on the basis of the points they score is irresistible. It is not unusual for young people to have the 'equivalent' of 12–15 GCSEs but without a C or above in English or maths ... (T)he young people themselves (and their parents) then expect to progress to a Level 3 qualification in FE ... but when they present at FE it is clear that their knowledge and understanding are poor. One sometimes wonders how much they have achieved ... (and) there is little option but to repeat a Level 2 qualification. (Wolf, 2010, pp. 80–81)

However, Wolf also found that most of those whose evidence she took wanted the continuation of some form of vocational or practical qualifications, hence her recommendation that up to 20% of the qualifications offered be vocational. This seemed to fly in the face of her acknowledgement that neither within the academic literature, nor within her own analysis, was there any indication that students at Key Stage 4, including specifically those at risk, i.e. the tail, made 'substantial improvement in their general attainment as a result of taking more vocational courses' (Wolf, 2010, 181). She also cited evidence that students drop out of vocational provision at the same rate as those who leave academic provision.

The underlying assumption, shared across the political spectrum, seems to be that up to 50% of children – not just the tail – have a 'style of learning' which is simply not compatible with the academic grind of GCSEs and A levels. Consequently – in the conventional wisdom – such students need more applied or vocational qualifications, and these must be the 'moral equivalents' of GCSEs or A levels. Our European counterparts do not share these peculiar notions; they insist that students in vocational programmes continue studying their native language, mathematics, social sciences and modern foreign languages. Yet in this country, we deny access to most academic subjects to those who have not gained five A*–C grades at age 16 – unless they resit GCSEs, a bleak endeavour indeed. The Coalition's EBacc is no remedy, since it concentrates once again on higher achievers. Schools will likely provide these subjects to those they believe are capable of getting the grades, rather than to all.

Officials and educational experts in this country have assumed that academic subjects are simply too boring for many students. But this is nonsense. Why should history be less exciting than leisure and tourism? Perhaps the answer is less in what we teach but, as Chris Husbands points out, in who teaches it, and to whom.

All students should have access to, and perhaps be required to study, the history of their country and another language besides English, as well as English, mathematics and science. This would return us to a more curriculum-centred offer as well as to what is often seen as a quaint notion of a broad and balanced curriculum. In order to address properly the 'it's just too boring' charge, we need better teachers, recruited from higher levels in the talent pool, and paid more than they now earn. As the House of Commons Education Select Committee has noted, very few of the best graduates become teachers; in 2007 those embarking on initial teacher-training averaged just 265 points on the UCAS tariff – the equivalent of three Cs at A level. In Finland, whose students lead the world on international tests, secondary school teachers have a minimum of an MA in the subject they teach. Their educational system *trusts* teachers; schools have far more autonomy than ours; there are no national tests before age 18; and within the limits of a basic national curriculum, teachers are free to teach as they see fit. But high academic achievement is not enough; teachers must also be passionate about what they teach and enthusiastic about sharing that passion with their students.

The current proposals for replacing GCSEs with EBCs, no matter whether or not you agree with norm-referenced linear qualifications assessed by three-hour examinations, will not do much to change the educational prospects of the tail. The changes will be *qualifications* reform, not *curriculum* reform. They will continue to provoke schools to try to game the system and the unintended consequences could be that schools give up even more than they already do on the bottom quintile, in their efforts to chase their slice of an already cut pie. Were this accountability picture changed to provide incentives to schools to enrol all students on EBC subjects regardless of outcomes, the bottom quintile could be inducted to the same cultural entitlement as their more privileged classmates. My biggest reservation about making such a recommendation is that on its own it is not sufficient. The bottom set is all too often relegated to learning through endless worksheets, copying from textbooks, watching videos and other mindless activities in order to keep them occupied. They don't need more of the same in a wider variety of subjects.

Aside from the measures that Chris Husbands advises need to be put in place to ensure that the teachers who have received the best training teach the bottom sets, the awarding body that is charged with writing, implementing and examining the new generation of awards that supersede the GCSEs must put in place teacher training specifically geared to teaching lower attainers, with this training supplemented by clear written guidance, support and tailored resources. This training needs to be supplemented by the schools themselves, preferably with all teachers collaborating on rigorous yet innovative ways of teaching students of all capabilities.

Reforms to teacher recruitment and retention policies such as those mentioned above will also go some way towards addressing these issues, but we will need a much deeper change too. We must nurture a culture that better respects the teaching profession and those who enter it, that sets great store by shared core knowledge and that values the education of *all* our children. In other words, we must rethink ruthlessly how, and especially what, our children learn.

## Policy implications

There is little political, or indeed cultural, appetite to shift from an examinations-driven education system to a curriculum-driven one. Our accountability system is predicated on how well (or otherwise) students do in their examinations, and the move to replace GCSEs with EBCs will do nothing to change that. Nothing in the current policy proposals will do anything to obviate the problem of the low expectations of the bottom 40–50% of pupils and they may indeed cause schools to focus even more fiercely on the minority of students who are likely to gain five 'good' grades in EBC qualifications. For the rest, there are hopeful statements about high aspirations for everyone and the end of the tiering system, but with no logical connection between those statements and policies that would actually help those in the tail. A statement of achievement for those for whom EBCs pose a challenge is a rather poor, second-rate substitute for what really counts.

If government was really serious about educating the tail it could:

- Return to a modified 1988 national curriculum model, where all students are *expected* to take English, mathematics, science, geography or history, an arts subject and a technology subject, with the last defined in a way that could, perhaps, include vocational options.
- If the first seems too radical, reintroduce the notion of an entitlement curriculum that all students would be *encouraged* to take and for which schools would receive incentives if students of all abilities accessed it.
- Change the accountability regime so that it rewarded more than high grades in certain qualifications, for example, by tying it into students' progress over time.

## References

Clifton, J. and Cook, W. (2012) 'A Long Division: Closing the Attainment Gap in England's Secondary Schools', London, IPPR.

DfE (2012) 'Twice As Many Students Now Taking Key Academic Subjects Thanks to the EBacc', http://www.education.gov.uk/inthenews/inthenews/a00215171/ebacc-means-twice-as-many-take-academic-subjects.

Harris, R. and Burn, K. (2011) 'Curriculum Theory, Curriculum Policy and the Problem of Ill-Disciplined Thinking', *Journal of Education Policy*, vol. 26, 2, pp. 245–261.

Higham, J. and Yeomans, D. (2007) 'Curriculum Choice, Flexibility and Differentiation 14–19: The Way Forward or Flawed Prospectus?', *London Review of Education*, vol. 5, 3, pp. 281–297.

LSIS (no date) 'Introduction to Foundation Learning', http://www.excellencegateway.org.uk/node/476.

National Society for Education in Art and Design (NSEAD) (no date) 'The Big Picture of the Secondary Curriculum', http://www.teachingcitizenship.org.uk/dnloads/bigpicture_sec_05_tcm8–157430.pdf

OECD (2010) *PISA 2009 Results: What Students Know and Can Do – Student Performance in Reading, Mathematics and Science (Volume I)*, available at http://dx.doi.org/10.1787/9789264091450-en

Rashid, Sammy and Brooks, Greg (2010) *The levels of Attainment in Literacy and Numeracy of 13- to 19-Year-Olds in England, 1948–2009*, London, NRDC.

Wolf, Alison (2011) *Review of Vocational Education – The Wolf Report*, London, DfE

Young, M. (2011) Education for a knowledge society, Or, The radical case for a subject-based curriculum. Draft conference paper, available at http://www.educonufs.com.br/ivcoloquio/conferenciademichaelyoung.pdf

# 9

# SEN and the tail

*Sophy Blakeway*

The Special Educational Needs regime is aimed at pupils who 'have a significantly greater difficulty in learning than the majority of children of the same age; or have a disability which prevents or hinders them from making use of educational facilities of a kind generally provided for children of the same age in schools within the area of the local education authority.'[1] This definition covers severe physical, sensory and neurological disorders, different levels of learning difficulties, as well as behavioural and other learning difficulties and syndromes such as dyslexia and attention-deficit hyperactivity disorder. Classifying pupils as Special Educational Needs (SEN) is the main way in which the allocation of additional resources to support physical and cognitive barriers to learning is formalised in England. Several levels of need are defined: School Action, School Action Plus, or (after a statutory assessment) a statement of SEN.

This chapter argues that in recent years many schools have reached too readily for the SEN label when faced with pupil underachievement, perpetuating a culture of low expectations which has too often trapped children in the tail of low attainment.[2] The UK is a clear outlier in terms of the proportion of students receiving additional support throughout compulsory schooling. Only the Netherlands and the USA have anything similar, and only at lower secondary age. In this context the extent of SEN classification in the UK seems excessive.

In 2010 OFSTED carried out a review into the issue which found that 'as many as half of all pupils identified for School Action [around 450,000 children] would not be identified as having special educational needs if schools focused on improving teaching and learning for all, with individual goals for improvement.' The review found: 'Around half the schools and early years provision visited used low attainment and relatively slow progress as their principal indicators of a special educational need.'[3]

Since 2006 the number of pupils with SEN[4] has increased from around 1.53 million (19% of pupils) to 1.67 million (21% of pupils) in 2011.[5] The number of pupils with statements of special educational needs (the most severe type of SEN) has actually decreased since 2003, whereas the numbers in School Action or School Action Plus categories increased, thus illustrating the very problem which OFSTED identified. As noted by Paul Marshall in Chapter 1, our SEN figure in this country is five times the EU average.

In 2010/11 the government spent almost £5.2 billion on SEN provision, £2.1 billion of which went to mainstream schools.[6] When a fifth of children are identified as having needs beyond normal mainstream schooling, it could be argued that there is something wrong, either with schools or with how the designation is being used.

In too many cases the SEN label has also become a proxy for socio-economic disadvantage. OFSTED found that 'pupils currently identified as having special educational needs are disproportionately from disadvantaged backgrounds, are much more likely to be absent or excluded from school, and achieve less well than their peers, both in terms of their attainment at any given age and in terms of their progress over time.'[7] Pupils with SEN are around twice as likely to be on free school meals as non-SEN children.[8]

The government's 2011 Green Paper on special educational needs reinforced OFSTED's conclusions, stating that 'too often the [SEN] label excuses inaction' and that 'this problem of over-identification sustains a culture of low expectations for these children and can mean that they do not get the right help.'[9]

The government admitted that the system of over-labelling has been caused in part by the perverse incentives associated with top-down performance measures. Although schools do not receive extra funding for School Action-classified children (some local authorities provide funding for School Action Plus), the use of contextual value-added performance measures has meant that schools' league table rankings have been boosted by having higher numbers of children with SEN. The system has inadvertently encouraged schools to include more children on the milder end of the SEN register, thereby raising the average attainment of the group and thus seemingly narrowing the gap between SEN and non-SEN students and giving the school a favourable score in public performance measures.

Clarity over the existence of flaws in SEN labelling now needs to be matched by action in addressing it. The government is committed to reforming SEN support through new legislation that, amongst other things, gives families greater control over the financial support they receive and reduces the number of school-based categories of special educational needs.

But government can only do so much. Informed by approaches being adopted across the ARK Schools network, this chapter looks at what schools can do to ensure *all* pupils make good progress and, in particular, focus on early academic intervention to accelerate the progress of low attainers to whom the SEN label has sometimes been too readily applied.

If there is a spectrum of need with pupils with severe learning difficulties at one end and low-attaining pupils with the most potential for acceleration at the other, there are those in the middle for whom categorisation is harder. Honesty and accuracy in diagnosis are critical to ensuring the right provision is made as soon as possible and the earlier this assessment happens in primary school the better. Over-hasty diagnosis of SEN for pupils with low attainment but the potential to improve with the right teaching and support leaves many at risk of demoralisation and in turn less likely to achieve.

## A question of identification

When identifying special educational needs, many schools focus on provision rather than pupil outcomes. Where this happens, schools will assign children to Code of Practice (COP) stages (School Action or School Action Plus) based on the provision made for them. So, for example, a school might assign all pupils who receive some kind of additional help – perhaps from teaching assistants, mental health workers or learning mentors – to either School Action or School Action Plus, whether their additional needs stem from learning difficulties or not. Rarely is the aim to accelerate the rate of progress. Rather, where students are underachieving, in the first instance schools should be asking what could be done to support them to make better progress. Schools often run catch-up sessions to enable this group of students to improve their attainment.

The same approach should be adopted for all students with low attainment. The COP suggests that schools should first target teaching approaches in the student's identified area of weakness. Some schools in the ARK Schools network do this very effectively: King Solomon Academy in north Westminster, for example, uses pre-teaching of concepts to low attainers to prepare them for new learning content and to ensure that those with low attainment have the necessary vocabulary to access the work. Those children who do not respond to this level of input are likely to have special educational needs and might need very different provision to be able to learn.

Another issue involves the lack of clarity around some categories of SEN. Behavioural, emotional and social difficulties (BESD) in particular is a very broad category and covers a whole range of difficulties, some of which may well be learning difficulties. Attention deficit hyperactivity disorder (ADHD), which can sometimes have a limiting impact on a pupil's ability to learn, is included in this category. The Pupil Support and Access guidance includes all of the following: 'Pupils with a range of difficulties, including emotional disorders such as depression and eating disorders; conduct disorders such as oppositional defiance disorder (ODD); hyperkinetic disorders including attention deficit disorder or attention deficit hyperactivity disorder (ADD/ADHD); and syndromes such as Tourette's, should be recorded as BESD if additional or different educational arrangements are being made to support them.' (Incidentally, the conditional clause here reinforces the unhelpful practice outlined above, whereby SEN is identified based on what provision is being made.)

While some difficulties related to BESD clearly can have a significant and long-term impact on learning, and therefore require special educational provision, often these types of difficulties need additional support that is unrelated to learning. For example, a student who struggles with social interaction with peers might need coaching from a school-based or external 'mentor' but their academic learning may be unaffected. Such children are often classified as having SEN because of the additional support they receive in school.

The difficulty of accurate or appropriate classification is perhaps best highlighted by the shift between primary and secondary school in the number of students assigned to different categories. The latest Department for Education data on SEN show that the most frequent type of primary SEN need is Speech, Language and Communication Needs (29.1%), followed by Moderate Learning Difficulties (21.8%) and BESD (18.6%); in secondary the most frequent primary needs are BESD (29%), MLD (22%) and Specific Learning Difficulties (15.9%). While the number of students with MLD remains relatively constant, there is a shift in the number identified with SLCN and BESD. Although arguably teenagers are much more difficult to manage than young children, the statistics seem to suggest significant differences in how primary and secondary schools classify SEN.[10]

A useful way of looking at SEN is to consider starting points and progress for individual students. Some schools use low attainment compared with the average attainment of same-age peers to identify special educational needs. The problem is that low attainment is not always the result of factors within the child; students who have not been exposed to quality teaching, for example, or whose specific areas of weakness have not been targeted early on, will necessarily lag behind their peers on measures of academic attainment. Furthermore, it is recognised that not all students develop at the same rate, meaning that variance in attainment is to be expected. The Code of Practice suggests that schools should use the rate of progress (as opposed to attainment level) as a key measure of whether students need additional support or not; the trigger for intervention at School Action, for example, is when students make little or no progress in spite of differentiated strategies targeted at their area of weakness.

## ARK Schools' approach: making catch-up mainstream

We do not claim that the ARK Schools model is perfect or that we have all the answers to this issue – indeed we know we have lots more to do – but we do believe that our educational ethos and practice is bringing real successes in raising attainment that could provide lessons for the wider education system.[11]

Our academies are generally situated in areas of high social deprivation, with twice the national average proportion of pupils with low attainment on entry.[12] Our philosophy of high expectations applies to all pupils and our educational model is underpinned by a firm belief that every child, including those with low prior attainment, can realise their potential with the right teaching and support. This overarching ethos is the key to everything we do in our schools and all the intervention programmes we run. It affects how we teach across the full age range – from Reception (where an early focus on literacy and numeracy helps reduce the likelihood of learning difficulties later on) to upper secondary. The ARK curriculum teaches pupils from their starting point, even if this is below the level normally expected in a given Key Stage, but is designed to achieve rapid catch-up for those students who are behind. All teaching and learning activity is integrated into the overall curriculum for pupils at every level – intervention and catch-up provision is not an 'afterthought'.

Practically, this manifests itself in a number of ways. The ARK curriculum prioritises depth before breadth, so that all pupils secure firm foundations in English and mathematics as the basis for all other parts of the curriculum. The ARK curriculum includes 12 hours of literacy a week in Key Stage 1, 10 in KS2 and 5 in KS3. Our primary literacy curriculum includes discrete spelling and handwriting lessons and at least 45 minutes of synthetic phonics a day until mastered, as well as regular out-loud class story reading. Early assessment of pupil needs is crucial for ensuring those with SEN are diagnosed as soon as possible, so all Year 1 children in ARK primary schools are screened for dyslexia through the Drive for Literacy programme.

Daily mathematics lessons in primary school are supplemented by 'mathematics meetings' where key facts and skills are practised to ensure fluency, often with rhymes and chants, and all secondary pupils study mathematics for at least five hours per week. ARK's Mathematics Mastery curriculum teaches fewer topics in greater depth to ensure that no child falls behind. Every concept or skill that is introduced is taught so that it is mastered by every child.

We recognise that good teaching for pupils with SEN usually benefits every child. For example, in mathematics teachers introduce concepts beginning with actual physical objects, move on to pictorial representations of the objects, and only once the pupils have a deep understanding are they introduced to the numeral or symbol that represents it. Building connections between different representations and manipulating objects in this way supports the mathematical understanding of every child, but has been shown to be particularly effective for pupils with SEN.

By operating a longer school day (typically 8.30 am to 4 pm in our primary schools and 8.30 am to 4.30 pm in our secondary schools) ARK academies are able to make time for catch-up while still providing a broad subject offer.

We have also had some successes in reducing the SEN roll of previously underperforming schools that have become ARK academies. Three out of the five ARK secondary academies that had

**Table 9.1: Percentage of pupils achieving level 2 by the end of Year 2 (2011/12)[13]**

|                    | *Reading* | *Writing* | *Maths* |
| ------------------ | --------- | --------- | ------- |
| ARK Schools network | 94%       | 91%       | 96%     |
| National           | 87%       | 83%       | 91%     |

replaced predecessor schools reduced their SEN numbers between 2009 and 2012. One transition primary, ARK Oval Primary Academy in Croydon, formerly a failing school that became an ARK academy in September 2011, has reduced its SEN register from 25% to 12% over one year by reviewing the categorisation of each child and distinguishing those who had been poorly taught from those with learning difficulties. The school has focused on providing concentrated catch-up for children previously identified as having SEN but who were low attainers in need of extra intervention.

For students whose attainment falls significantly outside typical variability in skills, knowledge and understanding, bespoke interventions are provided to speed up their progress and narrow the attainment gap within the school. Our schools use a number of different interventions to accelerate pupils' progress, including Catch Up Literacy and the LIT Programme, which targets pupils who start Year 7 at national curriculum level 2 or 3 for English (that is, one to two years behind the expected level) and aims to accelerate their reading and writing progress during the course of Year 7 so that they can achieve a minimum of level 4c by the end of the academic year. Most pupils respond well to these kinds of focused interventions, so it is possible to identify clear learning difficulties if children do not make progress through these extra programmes.

We are already seeing some notable successes. At primary level, our four schools with Key Stage 1 pupils in 2011/12 achieved results well above comparable national levels at the national benchmark of level 2.

## Progress of low attainers in ARK academies

Across the five ARK academies with GCSE results in 2011, the progress of low attainers was substantially ahead both of national and of academy averages.

- 78% of ARK pupils with low attainment on entry in Year 7 made the expected progress in English by KS4 compared with 52% nationally. In maths, two-thirds of low attainers made the expected progress compared with 29% nationally.
- Overall, ARK pupils with low attainment on entry in Year 7 are nearly four times as likely to achieve five A*–C GCSEs including English and maths as pupils nationally (35% versus 9%).

It is important to stress that this level of focus on low attainers is not at the expense of higher-ability children. In 2011, 93% of ARK high attainers made the expected progress in maths compared with 83% nationally (in English these figures are 92% and 85% respectively).[14]

## Conclusion/recommendations

At the public policy level, Ofsted's inspection framework needs to include an explicit focus on schools' success in improving the progress of low attainers and in moving children off the SEN register by targeted catch-up. If average attainment or average progress is used as a key indicator, a perverse incentive remains for schools to overuse SEN designations by including as many students as possible with low levels of need on their SEN register and thereby improve average attainment of the SEN group and narrow the gap with non-SEN pupils. Perhaps a better way of evaluating the quality of SEN provision would be to consider the progress made by specific groups of students, such as those with statements and those who arrived with below-average attainment levels, e.g. the progress of students who arrived in Year 7 with national curriculum level 1 in English/mathematics.

Changing the terminology would help too, with a category of Additional Educational Needs used to identify children who need some kind of extra support and intervention to ensure they make good progress.

Schools – particularly those in disadvantaged areas – should be acknowledged in OFSTED judgments for using the SEN label sparingly. This requires a cultural shift away from locating all issues around low attainment in the child and asking the hard but honest questions about how much of it is due to poor teaching. That way, schools will have a much clearer picture of which children have genuine learning difficulties requiring special provision, and be able to ensure they receive the appropriate level of help and support.

The government's commitment to replace the School Action and School Action Plus categories with a simpler new school-based category is welcome, as is the change in performance measures away from contextual value-added indicators towards displaying clear data on the progress levels of low, middle and high attainers. These changes must be underpinned by a fundamental shift in mindset within schools and matched by a similar shift in the accountability framework.[15]

With around 40% of 16-year-olds still falling short of the basic passport of five A*–C GCSEs including English and maths, we have much to do to raise attainment in this country. As part of this challenge, we must ensure SEN provision is focused on those who need it most and embed catch-up firmly within the mainstream curriculum so that teachers focus relentlessly on accelerating the progress of all pupils, particularly low attainers.

# 10

# Teaching and the tail: getting secondary school teachers in the right places doing the right things

*Chris Husbands*

For over 20 years, ever since examination league tables were first routinely published in England, policy makers, practitioners and parents have looked to them as a rough-and-ready indication of the variable quality of an education system. But we know now that the tables are by and large a reflection of the operation of out-of-school impacts on attainment. Those schools at the top of the tables – securing well above average results – are with a few notable and important exceptions schools in affluent communities, and those at the bottom are with a few important exceptions schools serving less affluent communities. Educational attainment and socio-economic status are very closely related in England: the outcomes of schooling are the outcomes, too often, of social inequality. This is one reason why, for example, the performance of schools in Richmond-upon-Thames appears to be so much better than the performance of schools in Kingston-upon-Hull: the schools in Richmond are educating more affluent children than the schools in Hull.

## Identifying the challenges

If this were the major challenge facing school improvement, a number of policy imperatives might suggest themselves. But, important though it is, it is not the only challenge. It turns out, despite the apparently obvious headline results, that it does not matter too much which school you go to. In the majority of schools, outcomes for individual pupils reflect the same socio-economic factors which drive outcomes across the system as a whole. In the vast majority of cases, children from less affluent homes will perform worse than children who are better off, whichever school they attend. In one, perhaps apocryphal story, a head teacher rightly boasted to a visiting politician that in his school there were 19% of pupils eligible for free school meals (FSM) – just above the then national average – but the school secured a well-above average of 81% scoring five A*–C GCSEs. It took the minister to point out that the 19% of pupils eligible for free school meals made up the 19% who failed to secure five A*–C GCSEs. Even in many successful schools, children from poorer backgrounds do not succeed.

The sheer scale of this pattern is summarised in a series of graphs compiled by Chris Cook of the *Financial Times*.[1] Figure 10.1 was created by giving every 16-year-old who took GCSEs at a state school in 2010 a point score for their exam performance: 8 points for an A* down to 1 point for a G. The scores were standardised, and then sorted based on IDACI codes measuring the level of poverty in each postcode area. The performance of children in deprived postcodes is at the left of the graph and the richest are at the right. As Chris Cook comments, 'if the school system were able to overcome all of a child's background, the line would be flat'. Where the data become more interesting is in comparison of the black line and the grey line. The grey line strips out schools which fall below the government's floor target of achieving at least 35% of pupils securing five A*–C GCSEs including English and mathematics – that is, the lowest-performing schools. The line barely moves, nor does it move when the threshold is shifted to 40%, 45%, 50% or above. These are devastatingly striking data.

Figure 10.1 **Pupil performance using all-GCSE measure**

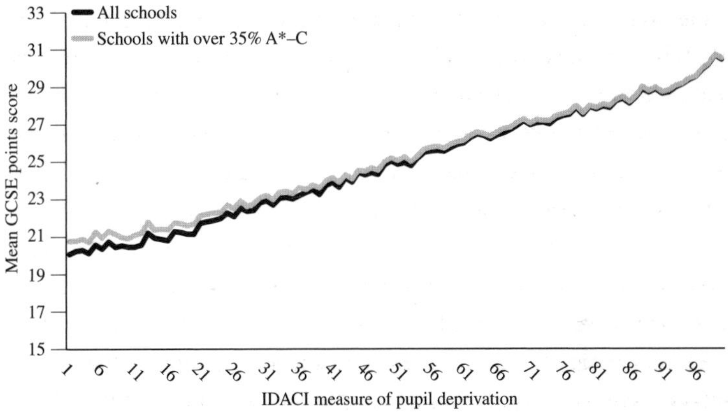

Source: National Pupil Database, via C. Cook (see note 1)

However, they do not show the whole picture. As Becky Allen[2] has shown, there are in fact some schools which are much more effective at closing the gap than most: schools with OFSTED 'outstanding' ratings for teaching and learning, producing high contextual value added, and which do manage to buck the trend and to close the gap between poor and better-off children. Indeed, as Sutton Trust analyses suggest, there are a relatively small number of schools where the educational outcomes for children on free school meals (FSM) are *better* than the average performance for children generally. These schools largely fall into two categories: there are a relatively large number where the numbers of FSM children are very small (a handful in each cohort), and a much smaller number where these numbers are very large. The second group of schools may benefit from being able to focus their systems on meeting the needs of FSM children at very high levels of quality. Ultimately, though, what these analyses tell us is that something else matters much more than which school you attend – and that's *who teaches you*.

None of this should be at all surprising across education systems.

There is an increasingly strong research and policy emphasis on the importance of teacher quality as a driver of outstanding educational outcomes. In overall system terms, the principle is explained in Michael Barber's now widely quoted aphorism: the quality of an education system cannot exceed the quality of its teachers.[3] In a similar vein, Bob Schwartz, in a summary of evidence on educational reform, argues that 'the most important school-related factor in student learning ... is teaching',[4] whilst Fenton Whelan draws together the system evidence to conclude that 'school systems need to ensure that their curricula are relevant and contain enough flexibility to accommodate different learners and different social and economic needs. They need to ensure that school buildings are in good condition ... All these things are important, and ultimately impact academic performance. However, none is nearly as important as the quality of teaching'.[5] Ben Levin, explaining 'how to change five thousand schools', is clear that the 'heart of school improvement rests in improving daily teaching and learning practices in schools'.[6] As a result, school systems across the world have begun to be impatient about overall levels of teacher quality. Steve Machin, writing about the English evidence for the Sutton Trust, concludes that 'having a very effective, rather than an average, teacher raises each pupil's attainment by a third of [an examination] grade ... Bringing the lowest-performing 5–10% of teachers in the UK up to the average would greatly boost attainment and lead to a sharp improvement in the UK's international ranking'.[7] The problem in England is partly one of teacher quality – we are only now taking seriously the need to attract, systematically, the brightest and the best to the profession. But it is also about deployment: across our school system the best teachers are in the wrong places – at both the level of the school and the classroom.

**Teacher deployment**

Outstanding teaching can make a really significant contribution to raising the performance of the tail, closing gaps in attainment and improving life chances, but too few outstanding teachers are in the places where they can make that difference. The American evidence adduced by Ronfeldt et al.[8] suggests that in the most challenging schools, high levels of teacher turnover compound the problems. It is even arguable that what makes the difference between more advantaged and less advantaged schools is as much about staffing stability – retaining satisfactory and better teachers for substantial periods of time – as the ability to recruit individual teachers of particular quality. There are macro- and micro-level incentives which systematically divert the best teachers from the places they can do the most good. At the macro level, the teacher labour market diverts teachers to the more successful schools. Unusually by international standards, we have a very open teacher labour market in which teachers are appointed to individual schools – this was a feature of the English system long before the introduction of local management of schools. In most of England, the strong relationship between socio-economic performance and educational outcomes means that more advantaged schools are more attractive to teachers as places to work; good teachers by and large migrate to good schools. Equally important are the incentives for the deployment of teachers within schools. Generally speaking, it is in schools' interests to deploy the best teachers in teaching the most advantaged groups. This incentive is driven largely by performance measures, and the influence of league tables on the in-school deployment of teachers is considerable. Under current accountability mechanisms it is in schools' interests to deploy teachers in teaching *either* those pupils who are on the cusp of borderline performance measures (GCSE pupils at the D/C borderlines, or primary pupils in Year 6) *or* at the very top of the examination and attainment range. These incentives coincide with a deep cultural tradition in English secondary grammar and independent schools where the practice was for the 'senior master'– the most experienced and senior teacher in the department – to teach the most advantaged examination groups. Curiously, there is some American research evidence to suggest that teacher effectiveness is actually more important in determining out-comes at lower levels of the attainment and motivation range.[9] Put like this, the challenge for teacher deployment is twofold: the devel-opment of incentives to recruit and *retain* effective teachers in the most challenging schools, but also, once they are there, to develop in-school incentives to deploy them more effectively.

Left to itself, the school system will not correct for these prob-lems. Left to itself, and with performance indicators which encourage schools to focus on the needs of higher-attaining and more advan-taged students, the teacher labour market will by and large do what it is already doing in terms of reinforcing inequalities through teacher deployment. The teacher labour market is not working; it is not incen-tivising excellent teachers to be deployed in those schools where they can make a real difference. Teacher recruitment and deploy-ment practices need intervention to correct for market tendencies. In practice, there has been some experience of using market signals to attract teachers to more challenging schools: between 2006 and 2009, the Training and Development Agency for Schools used a system of 'golden hello' payments to attract newly trained teachers to schools facing challenging circumstances. Although the programme had some successes, the labour market signals it sent – a payment of £6,000 after teachers had worked in one of the designated schools for three years – were probably not strong enough. Teach First, the innovative employ-ment-based training route which places high-potential graduates in challenging schools for two years, has been much more effective as a redistributive mechanism for the deployment of *high-potential gradu-ates*. The available data do not, as yet, allow us to unpick the impact of these teachers on overall effectiveness for a number of reasons: first, because we lack the data to relate the impact of individual teachers or groups of teachers on school level attainment, secondly because in many cases Teach First participants are staffing previously under-staffed schools, and thirdly because we know almost nothing about the deployment of high-potential teachers *within* schools. Moreover, the Teach First 'offer' places a strong emphasis on the two-year tour of duty and relatively little emphasis on retention within challenging schools. To be effective, policy needs to be more sophisticated and realistic about the level of rewards which would be needed to attract and retain the most successful teachers in the most challenging schools; more than this, policy needs to develop signals which encourage staffing stability in challenging schools. The TDA scheme of £6,000 offered, effectively, a salary enhancement of £40 per week before tax, with no performance element which rewarded success. Teach First, for all its success in *deploying* graduates in schools, is in some ways a potential contributor to a further problem for challenging schools – the problem of staff turnover.

## Deployment policy packages

In practice, it is unlikely that any level of retention-based award would be sufficiently well focused to achieve its aims, since it has few long-term accountability measures. There are alternative ways to think about the challenge, though both involve significant changes to the way the teacher labour market operates in English schools. In this chapter, I outline two policy packages which could produce step changes in the way teachers are deployed between and within schools to make a real impact on the attainment of the tail. The first, the **Teaching Priority Programme**, would be focused on attracting teachers at whatever salary level to designated schools. Designated schools for this programme would be those schools with above twice the average proportion of pupils eligible for free school meals, those in the lower quartile of schools nationally for mean prior attainment, and those with more than twice the number of pupils in the lowest quartile of attainers. Schools would be eligible to apply for participation in the Teaching Priority Programme for five years; in practice, the criteria are likely to apply to something like one quarter of schools. The purpose of the programme would be to attract teachers to work in these schools. The package would comprise three main elements:

a salary supplement for newly recruited teachers beginning at £3,000 for the first year, rising to £4,500 in the second year, to £6,500 in the third year and stabilising at £8,000 in the fourth and subsequent years. This supplement would be met by government and would not be a charge on the school's own budget. The second element would be a professional development guarantee, offering teachers a voucher to be redeemed against professional development opportunities and, like the salary supplement, rising over the period of time during which the teacher is on the payroll of the school – beginning at £500 for the first year and rising to £1,000, £1,500 and £2,000 in successive years. The final element, in addition to the first two, would be a modest performance-related amount on salary based not on the average examination performance of the pupils taught by the teacher but on the performance of FSM pupils taught by the teacher. After five years in the Teaching Priority Programme, teachers would be eligible for a fully funded one-term sabbatical. The overall cost of the programme over five years would be the equivalent of one additional teaching salary for one year. Put differently, amortised over the five-year period, the cost represents a 20% premium on teaching salary costs for every teacher recruited into the Teaching Priority Programme. Set against this there would be significant short-term and longer-term savings: lower staffing turnover in otherwise hard-to-staff schools would present a modest source of savings. Irrespective of savings, the overall cost of the TPP over five years, assuming the deployment of 10,000 teachers to TPP schools, would be in the region of £500m.

Taken as a whole, the **Teaching Priority Programme** would act as a powerful incentive for teachers to work in the most challenging schools. However, one potential weakness of the TPP is that it could also act as an incentive for both weaker and stronger teachers to be deployed into the programme. For this reason, in addition to a school eligibility element there would need to be a teacher eligibility element. Teachers would need to apply to participate, so that the scheme could attract the most effective among them. Application for admission to the TPP could draw on a range of data sources, setting appropriate entry requirements. It would not be possible or sensible to use previous successful experience in a similar setting as a principal entry requirement, not least because the TPP is intended to attract teachers to work in hard-to-staff schools. However, the extensive experience of, for example, Teach First and NPQH (National Professional Qualification for Headship) in selecting high-potential candidates suggests that assessment centres can be devised which identify those most likely to be effective. Moreover, a key advantage of the TPP is that it does something which Teach First has hitherto failed to do: essentially, Teach First is a selection device for identifying high-potential new graduates; the TPP would identify high-potential experienced teachers. The TPP would have the potential to change the way teacher career structures are conceived.

One of the features of the teacher labour market in England is its high degree of fracture. Essentially, we have 22,000 employers in a competitive labour market, or, more accurately, 4,000 secondary and 18,000 primary employers. There are enormous strengths in such a labour market, which is, potentially at least, highly flexible and effectively embeds school autonomy. But that autonomy and resulting fragmentation, and the highly uneven structure of the market, build in some absurd inefficiencies, at local and system level. There is no strategic basis for deploying teachers across the system; there are no incentives for sharing scarce expertise; there are no incentives for exploring radical or innovative deployment models for teachers cross-phase – for example, modern languages teachers who might work across primary and secondary schools, or expert physics teachers who might work across a number of secondary schools. In practice, some deployment of teachers across schools has begun to work. The emergence of National Leaders of Education, Local Leaders of Education and, more recently, of Specialist Leaders of Education has begun to shift the way teacher expertise is conceived: NLEs, LLEs and now SLEs work on coaching, mentoring and in advisory ways in a range of schools, increasingly in alliances of teaching schools. Their expertise has proved valuable in turning round poor school leadership performance or under-performing departments within schools. As groups of academies emerge, some with employment contracts held at the level of the group, it is likely that greater use will be made of LLEs and SLEs to support schools and teachers facing challenges.

The proposal which follows draws on, but extends, the work of NLEs/LLEs and SLEs to develop more fluid models for the teacher labour market which I identify as **Teaching Priority Areas**. These would be groups of schools in areas of severe social and economic disadvantage, with patterns of underperformance across the groups which are similar to those identified in the TPP. The purpose of the TPAs would be to identify geographical areas where intensive and continuing support could make a significant difference. Schools in the designated TPA would be able to establish a joint employment vehicle to supply experienced and high-quality teachers to the cluster on the same basis as the TPP. In effect, a cluster of schools in, say, a coastal town or part of a borough would pool elements of their staffing budget to purchase a team of teachers against agreed criteria and these teachers would be deployed across the group of schools. This would have several advantages over current practices. First, it would mean that particular high-quality expertise could be deployed across an area – for example, specialist expertise in raising standards for boys in mathematics. Secondly, by locating the resource at area rather than school level it would require schools to think collectively about how to deploy the expertise in the most effective way across the group of schools. In many cases, emerging academy groups are deploying staffing resources flexibly across the group. But given the complex geography which is emerging, it remains likely that resources will be fractured and ineffective. It could be that the development of **Teaching Priority Areas** would see the emergence of a number of providers of groups of high-quality staff to the TPAs; such providers might include groups of teachers themselves, universities, school chains or charities. These providers would be able to establish Teacher Partnership Groups which would employ teachers and then deploy them into

Teaching Priority Areas on the same basis as the Teaching Priority Programme. The model would allow teachers to work in teams across schools and would allow, say, a highly skilled maths teacher to work across four or five secondary schools engaged substantially in teaching pupils but also in coaching and mentoring staff. However, it would leave individual schools in control of overall staffing and deployment within the schools – something that also needs addressing.

## Additional measures

Taken together, the **Teaching Priority Programme** and the development of **Teaching Priority Areas** will begin to transform the teacher labour market to improve supply and retention of teachers in schools facing challenging circumstances. On their own, they will make a difference. However, what they will not *necessarily* address are the performance indicator signals which impact on in-school deployment. There are a number of additional measures which need to be deployed in order to maximise the impact of these proposals on pupils at the lower end of the attainment range, and to shift perceptions about in-school deployment. The development of Teacher Partnership Groups could provide a mechanism for changing deployment patterns, since contracts could be constructed to secure appropriate deployment: a cluster of schools could contract with a Teacher Partnership Group to deploy teachers with particular groups or to impact on the outcomes of particular groups of children. For example, a Teacher Partnership Group could be contracted specifically to deploy teachers in a group of schools to close the gap between the highest- and lowest-performing groups of pupils or to raise the performance of pupils on free school meals. In this way, the contract with the Teacher Partnership Group could be a mechanism for spending pupil premium funds to secure improved outcomes for disadvantaged learners. More generally, however, government needs to acknowledge the extent to which the current performance tables reinforce in-school deployment strategies which actively militate against raising the performance of the most disadvantaged young people.

Some progress has been made, with revisions to performance tables. Secondary school GCSE attainment data are now presented separately for groups of low- (below level 4 at KS2), middle- (level 4 at KS2) and high- (above level 4 at KS2) attaining pupils, and such approaches are likely to encourage desirable behaviour from schools by prompting them to focus on attainment of all pupils, rather than the marginal grade C/D borderline pupils, and to deploy teaching staff appropriately. Unfortunately, as Becky Allen has observed, this largely positive measure has been undermined by the particular way it has been implemented by government, which has chosen to report average attainment across quite a large group of pupils, with up to 45% of pupils in the middle band. Because the *group* of pupils is large, the indicator 'simply replicates the problems of reporting "raw" GCSE attainment: more affluent schools will appear to do better than more deprived schools, at least in part because their prior ability distribution is more favourable'.[10] Allen and Burgess offer a different measure, reporting attainment by group but making the size of the groups small: a low-attainment group scoring in the 20th–30th percentile at Key Stage 2; a middle-attainment group scoring in the 45th–55th percentile; and a high-attainment group scoring in the 70th–80th percentile. Focusing on these much smaller groups would enable a clearer sense of how a school is performing for different groups of pupils. Of course, it is naive to suppose that something so technical will have a serious impact on the management of school performance tables, but one strong possibility would be to make performance on these criteria a limiting factor in OFSTED inspection grades, so that a school could not be 'outstanding' for pupil attainment if its indicators on all three groups were not outstanding. Such a development would strongly incentivise secondary schools to deploy their teaching staff in ways which raised the attainment of all pupils.

Enormous advances have been made in school performance over the past 20 years but the strong link between socio-economic status and educational performance has not been broken, and in many cases has been reinforced. In the 1960s and 1970s, it was argued that a principled public policy approach to the relationship between school make-up and performance would be to enforce school mixing through 'bussing'. The emergence of school choice as a powerful ideological driver within the school system means that it is no longer politically possible to think in terms of widespread pupil movement – although there remain calls, notably from the Sutton Trust, for arrangements to open up high-performing private schools to poor but able pupils. Since we appear to have abandoned the idea that pupils will be allocated more equitably between schools, the other principal resource we have to deploy are teachers. But the teacher labour market and the operation of performance indicators are not working for the most disadvantaged learners and radical approaches are needed. In this chapter I have explored two sets of policy interventions which might make a difference: strong intervention in the teacher labour market to incentivise teachers to work in the most disadvantaged schools, and to stay there, and interventions to encourage deployment of the best teachers across clusters of schools. I have also considered shifting the focus on school inspection to encourage novel approaches to in-school deployment of teachers. The current approach we have to teacher deployment is effectively a market failure: the operation of the labour and school management market is reinforcing negative outcomes for the most disadvantaged. [11]

# 11

## Talent and the tail: getting the highest-quality teaching and leadership into our most challenging schools

*James Toop*

The quality of teaching and leadership in schools is the key factor in raising student achievement. For a child from a disadvantaged background, the difference between a good teacher and a poor teacher is one year's learning.[1] That is at least one GCSE grade. Spread across five teachers, and it is the difference between a child achieving five Ds at GCSE and five Cs. The difference between outstanding and inadequate leadership is stark. From OFSTED data, McKinsey found that for every 100 schools with good leadership and management, 93 will have good standards of student achievement, but for every 100 schools that do not, only one will have these good standards.[2]

We have made significant progress over the past ten years in raising floor standards, but our results continue to show a strong correlation between socio-economic background and student achievement.[3] We still have a long tail and wide achievement gap present within the majority of schools.[4] The positive news is that there are schools bucking this trend and showing that the tail can be reduced. For example, Wembley High School in Brent and Perry Beeches in Birmingham have shown that the achievement gap can be reduced to

8% and 7% respectively compared with a national gap of 27%.[5] The key factor in their success has been the relentless pursuit to recruit, develop and retain high-quality teachers and leaders.

Increasing numbers of examples exist at a micro-level, but there appear to be three core reasons impacting the quality of teaching and leadership across the wider system:

1. Supply: teaching is not seen as a high-status profession and we struggle to attract the best graduates. Once in the profession, we struggle to develop and promote them, leading to low retention. Sixty-six per cent of graduates feel that teaching offers slow career progression and promotion rates[6] and only 74% of newly qualified teachers remain in teaching five years later, citing lack of professional development as one of the main reasons for leaving.[7]

2. Deployment: it is a challenge to attract the best teachers to work in schools with the highest need. Part of this challenge is related to geography, and evidence in Chapter 3 that the tail is largest in regional, rural and coastal areas outside London.[8] And part is related to socio-economic disadvantage; only 10% of teachers want to work in the most challenging schools.[9] Teachers and leaders are not incentivised to work there as career progression is often judged on experience in a school rated 'outstanding' by OFSTED rather than success in more challenging schools.

3. Variable teacher quality: all schools have some good teachers but they do not all have enough. It would seem that we lack consistent quality teaching in every classroom in every school as 55% of the variation in achievement in our system comes from variations in student performance within schools.[10]

The impact of improvements in teaching and leadership across the system could be huge and it may only require an incremental improvement. Bringing the lowest-performing 10% of teachers in the UK up to the average would greatly boost attainment and lead to a sharp improvement in the UK's international ranking. In five years the UK's rank amongst OECD countries could improve from 21st in reading to as high as 7th, and from 22nd in maths to as high as 12th. Over ten years (the period a child is in the school system before the PISA examinations) the UK would improve its position to as high as 3rd in reading and 5th in maths.[11]

In this chapter I will explore three potential solutions to the challenge of raising the quality of teaching and leadership:

1. Increase supply of talent: attract the best graduates into teaching and then develop them into outstanding leaders who stay in the most challenging areas and schools.
2. Deploy innovatively: focus the best teachers and leaders on the schools with the highest need, achieving a critical mass in those schools to reach a tipping point in student results.
3. Build ripple effect: utilise the best teachers and leaders to develop and inspire other teachers to get to 'good', especially the bottom 10%.

## The Talent Solution: growing and retaining talent within the system

The first step in increasing the talent supply is to attract the best graduates into teaching. International systems, such as those in Korea and Finland, have achieved this by raising the status of teaching. They raised entry standards to teaching through higher degree standards, selection through a four-stage competency-based assessment process and increasing financial incentives for graduates in specific subjects. In the 2010 White Paper,[12] the UK government introduced initiatives aimed at the same goal, raising the minimum degree grade eligible for funding to a 2:1, and introducing bursaries for shortage subjects. The recent Education Select Committee report[13] also raised the idea of a College of Teaching to further enhance the profession's status.

Government has also sought to give the schools more control over professional development by introducing Teaching Schools.

However, one of the most impactful initiatives to date in increasing the supply and availability has come from three not-for-profit charities: Teach First, Teaching Leaders and Future Leaders. They all identify, train and develop high-potential teachers and leaders, building a spine of skills through the system, but interestingly, it is not financial incentives or career development which motivate participants on the programmes.

What unites them is a shared vision that socio-economic background should not predict a child's future success and a focus on schools in the most challenging contexts. They feel part of a wider movement to address educational disadvantage and they are also selective, turning away large numbers of graduates and school leaders every year. The Select Committee highlighted the rigour of the assessment process, which is competency based, identifying potential to lead rather than existing experience, to select applicants on to their programmes to ensure they recruit the highest-quality participants.[14] It is worth noting that several Academy chains, such as ARK, United Learning and Oasis, have similar mission-driven approaches which are increasingly attracting the best teachers who want to have an impact on educational disadvantage.

Since 2002, the three programmes have collectively recruited, trained and developed 4,000 teachers, 484 middle leaders and 350 senior leaders, and currently have 32 head teachers. The impact on the mission through pupil achievement in their schools has been significant. Teach First received an OFSTED outstanding judgement for its teachers. Teaching Leaders' departments have increased GCSE A\*–C rates by an average 15% over the two-year development programme, and schools led by a Future Leaders headteacher have increased five A\*–C passes by 6.5% on average in 2012.

Given the selective process, one question is how far the three programmes can go in addressing their mission across the (approximately) 1,200 eligible schools.[15] At current annual levels (1,000 teachers, 300 middle leaders, 75 senior leaders), momentum is building, but a significant increase would be required across Teach First and Teaching Leaders to achieve system-wide impact across challenging schools. At the current scale 50% of all challenging school heads could be Future Leaders by 2020, but Teach First would need to grow to 5,000 teachers annually, and Teaching Leaders would have to train 1,500 middle leaders annually to reach that target.

There is a question about whether this growth is achievable. One proof point is Teach for America (TFA), which now recruits 5,000 teachers annually, impacting 750,000 children. Teach First could mirror its growth trajectory. TFA is 20 years old, exactly ten years on from where Teach First is now. In its first ten years it recruited 1,000 teachers, but most of its exponential growth came in years 15 to 20. To match this pattern, Teach First would need to reach 2,500 by 2017 and 5,000 by 2022. Teaching Leaders currently has 215 Fellows in its 2012 intake and targets 330 for 2013. There are 30,000 middle leaders in eligible schools so at similar growth rates to Teach First it would be possible to reach 1,500 annually. This would represent 5% of middle leaders, which increases impact but also retains the focus on the leaders with the highest potential.

Government would need to continue to invest and grow all three programmes. At present, the programmes leverage large amounts of external funding, have developed economies of scale and have reduced and are committed to further reducing their reliance on government funding, but it would be unrealistic for them to exist without government support. For example, in 2011, Teach First was 55% government-funded (£9.2m of total income of £16.6m);[16] in 2012, Teaching Leaders is 60% government-funded (£3m of total income of £5m); and in the same year, Future Leaders received further government expansion funding. Evidence from the OECD points to the fact that directing funding to teaching and leadership offers the best return on investment for student outcomes, so relative to the impact of other school improvement strategies they offer good value for money.[17] The other significant challenge may be balancing the need to reach growth targets against maintaining the quality of the participants, which is a factor that initially made the programmes attractive and successful.

A first proposal to reduce the tail is for the programmes and government to develop a ten-year system-wide strategy to build a talent pipeline and get the best teachers and leaders into schools with the highest need. Government should work with and fund Teach First, Teaching Leaders and Future Leaders to define and achieve this with long-term goals, but also explore other new innovative policies which link existing policies, such as financial incentives and career progression, to working in the most challenging schools. One example of this could be what is happening in the city of Shanghai, where the school leaders can only progress to a Principal role if they can demonstrate impact in a challenging school. The result might focus existing teachers and leaders on areas where the tail is greatest.

**Innovation: deploying talent more effectively to reduce the tail**

The talent pipeline is part of the solution but it is likely to take time to build this pool. As this grows, another solution might be to think innovatively about how to deploy and utilise the currently available talent in the most effective way. The first part of the challenge at a system level is geography, as there appears to be a correlation between areas with long tails of underachievement and challenges in recruiting and attracting the best teachers and leaders. In 2011, Teaching Leaders worked with a group of head teachers in Hastings and Brighton to launch a small cohort on the south coast and their key motivator was to retain their best teachers and raise the prestige of teaching in the towns.

One solution to this problem of geography has been for high-performing schools to support other schools in the same geography, by sharing and deploying talent across schools to improve results and reduce variation between them. The City Challenge initiatives, in particular London Challenge and National Leaders of Education (NLEs), have been particularly effective in brokering and building collaboration between school leaders with strong results. Teaching Schools is a new intervention, still at an early stage, which aims to replicate this school-to-school support, but with schools taking the leading role. Academy chains are also increasingly using their network effect to provide support across schools through cross-chain development programmes and mentoring.

This solution has worked in areas where Academies and schools are more closely clustered, and has been one of the key reasons for the success of the Harris academy chain, which has focused on narrow clustering to allow school-to-school support to flourish. However, this becomes more challenging when you move out of the major conurbations, London, Manchester and Birmingham, which were the early focus of the City Challenge initiatives. Outside these areas, schools are more isolated both geographically and in terms of local networks.

As we saw above, much of the variation in teacher quality appears to exist within schools. Therefore, as well as looking at how we use the principles of City Challenge and NLEs to share and distribute talent to increase school-to-school support, one option to consider further is how we can increase the supply and retention of talent to individual schools located in the most challenging geographies. Applying the talent solution at the micro-level, we could explore a strategy focused on building a critical mass of high-quality teachers and leaders in an individual school to achieve a tipping point both in talent and in student results.

Some schools are already pursuing this strategy informally. They have been working strategically with Teach First, Teaching Leaders and Future Leaders to build a critical mass of talent. Over the past decade, Mulberry School in Tower Hamlets has built a cohort of 24 Teach First teachers and in 2011 achieved 78% five A*–C GCSEs, including English and maths. Similarly, over the past five years Greenford High School in Ealing has worked extensively with Teach First and Future Leaders and has ten Teaching Leaders Fellows; in 2011, its GCSE results increased to 72% A*–C, including English and maths.

Taking this idea further, joining up and integrating the deployment of the Teach First, Teaching Leaders and Future Leaders solutions within specific individual schools could provide an interesting way of achieving this critical mass. At the planning level, this would require the programmes and the school to have early-stage, joined-up, strategic conversations. These conversations would focus on placing and training a critical number of participants, built up over a multi-year period, and ensuring they work together. This would allow them to focus on specific strategic interventions integrated at all levels of leadership in the school, resulting in a significant impact on raising achievement and a reduction in the tail.

This could be extremely cost-effective as a school improvement strategy. As an example, investing in three Teach First teachers, three Teaching Leaders Fellows, and one Future Leader, with wider middle and senior leadership training across the school, could be achieved for around £20,000–25,000 per year. If the talent was retained, as with Mulberry and Greenford, within 3 years and at a cost of £60,000–70,000 there could then be a critical mass of talent in the school at all levels. To put it into context, this would mean recruiting, retaining and developing over 25 teachers, for an amount far lower than the advertising, interviewing and cover costs to recruit that number of staff.

The combined effect provides an interesting strategic human capital solution to school improvement. With funding from the Education Endowment Foundation, Teach First, Teaching Leaders and Future Leaders are about to embark on a three-year project, Achieve Together, with 24 schools in specific areas with high levels of socio-economic challenge to test the collective impact of Teach First, Teaching Leaders and Future Leaders. Through this project, we will test different deployment and coordination models to see what is most effective, but it raises the interesting option that the strategic deployment of high-quality teachers and leaders could be a human capital solution to school improvement.

A second proposal is that schools could invest in Teach First, Teaching Leaders and Future Leaders as a combined human capital solution to school improvement, and the organisations should strategically direct their participants to areas of high need and focus on building a critical mass of leaders in individual schools rather than spreading too thinly across many schools. Further research is required to calculate how many outstanding teachers, middle leaders and senior leaders are needed to reach a critical mass to improve a school and reduce the tail. But the Education Endowment Foundation project provides an opportunity to understand how to apply this human capital solution and could provide an interesting model for joining up the work of Teach First, Teaching Leaders and Future Leaders further.

## Building the ripple: leveraging the impact of talent to develop and inspire other teachers

Placing a disproportionate number of talented teachers and leaders in the most challenging schools would leave us with a critical mass of mission-driven, high-quality individuals concentrated in the schools with the highest need. When combined with the first solution of growing the talent pool at a system level, this would give us more, in terms of volume and concentration of talent, but could still leave two gaps.

We would have more high-quality teachers and leaders, but still not enough in all high-need schools and geographies. For example, there will be schools with a strong head and teachers in certain departments, but weak heads of department across the school, or there may be individual schools in certain areas that we cannot fully reach. Therefore, the next option to explore is how we could get more value from this new talent pool in the schools and areas where we do not have the critical mass. Essentially, by investing in creating this talent pool, we could expect more from teachers. The investment could be leveraged to create a ripple effect, getting teachers to direct their focus beyond their area of responsibility, and so develop and inspire other colleagues in their school. The idea would be to create a tipping point in teacher quality and get every teacher and lesson to 'good'.

Where this ripple effect could have the greatest impact is with the bottom 10% of teachers, but this group is hard to reach and engage. A minority of teachers within this group do not want to change and it is right for schools to use their powers to remove them from the classroom. The rest are not able to improve at present but want to, and they need the re-energising, development and self-belief to become more effective. If we could use high-quality leaders in the system to operate as effective line managers, coaches and peer mentors, targeting their time and support at the bottom 10%, it might be possible to leverage the investment in their training to improve this hard-to-reach group. At a system level, there are roughly 10,000 teachers who would fall into the bottom 10% of teachers in challenging schools. To address this group we would need to develop only 3,000 to 5,000 effective middle leaders, assuming each develops 2–3 members of staff.

It would also be interesting to explore applying the Shanghai practice discussed above to career progression for leaders in schools. Taking the model to lower levels of leadership, we could make the development of underperforming staff a prerequisite of promotion in the future to a middle or senior leadership role. Strong 'developing others' and 'holding to account' competencies are two of the means by which higher- and lower-scoring candidates at Teaching Leaders and Future Leaders assessment centres are differentiated. Teaching Leaders integrates staff development into its two-year programme for high-potential middle leaders. We ask middle leaders to identify members of their team to develop and we monitor their impact based on the improvements in teacher quality and student outcomes of the staff being developed. If all aspiring middle and senior leaders had to demonstrate and show evidence of their impact on other staff as part of their career progression, then we could shift the culture towards spreading impact within schools.

With this in mind, a third proposal would be to link career progression of high-potential leaders to experience and impact in the most challenging schools. As a prerequisite before promotion, teachers and leaders would need to demonstrate impact on closing the gap and reducing the tail, and evidence of developing and turning around underperforming staff in those schools. There are currently 1,200 secondary schools that meet this criterion, meaning nearly 100,000 teaching posts, 30,000 middle leadership roles and 1,200 head teacher posts. Given current recruitment levels to the three programmes of 1,000 teachers, 300 middle leaders and 75 senior leaders, there would still be enough posts to make this easily feasible. This could be achieved in a minimum of two years at each level, but would incentivise and focus the best teachers and leaders on wanting to work in schools with high levels of socio-economic deprivation.

The effectiveness of teachers and leaders represents one of our best chances of reducing the tail across the system. If we could get every teacher to 'good', in a decade we would be at the top end of the PISA tables. Three potential solutions exist but each has limitations. We can increase supply of top talent by growing existing Teach First, Teaching Leaders and Future Leaders programmes, but such rapid growth may not be compatible with quality. We can experiment with new models of how we deploy talent to reach the critical mass of high-quality teachers and leaders needed to achieve a tipping point and reduce the tail in an individual school, but we are at an early stage and more research will be required. Finally, we could leverage the investment in developing these high-quality leaders to create a ripple effect to develop and inspire the bottom 10%, but this is a challenging process and difficult to manage. Whilst it may be slow to begin with, this change is like the flywheel which Jim Collins describes in 'Good to great'. It takes a little while to get going but once momentum builds the movement grows exponentially and becomes unstoppable. This will increase quality, motivation and retention, meaning that the investment remains in the system and grows over a sustained period of time, giving us a real chance of shifting the tail of educational underachievement.

# 12

# Incentives for educating the tail

*Dale Bassett[1]*

The English school system is very effective at determining schools' behaviour. The quasi-market, which is really a system of centrally prescribed incentives put in place by government, drives this. The government says it wants schools to achieve a particular target – say, 50% of pupils getting five grade Cs or better at GCSE – and that's what it gets. Schools fall over themselves to bow to the will of ministers. Through relentless work, excellent teaching and some shrewd qualification selection, schools deliver. But these incentives simply do not exist for the 20% of children who leave 12 years of compulsory education with nothing.

## Success for the many at the expense of the few

At the heart of this problem is the system of targets put in place by government to create incentives for schools. The way in which we define underperformance has a major impact on what schools actually do – and, crucially, which pupils they focus their efforts on. Since 2005, the government's chosen measure has been the percentage of children in each school who get at least five 'good' GCSEs (i.e. grade C or higher) including English and maths. The Coalition government has raised the threshold from 30% to 40%, and it will rise to 50% in 2014.

This 'floor standard' has worked: schools have increased the number of their children hitting this benchmark. More children than ever are leaving the school system with at least these five good GCSEs. Schools that fall below the floor standard are subject to intervention, and since 2000 this has often come in the form of 'academisation'. Persistently underperforming schools are converted to 'academy' status – meaning they are given more freedoms than normal schools – and put under the care of a sponsor organisation, often a charity such as ARK that has a good record of turning difficult schools around.

This has been widely regarded as a success, and the hundreds of schools that have become sponsored academies have been largely responsible for the significant fall in the number of chronically underperforming schools in England over the past decade. Indeed, the success of the first generation of 'sponsored' academies was the prompt for the Coalition government extending to all schools the option to convert to academy status, to take advantage of the same freedoms. 'Free schools' – new academies set up by groups of parents or teachers – are intended to do much the same thing, as well as spur competition between schools to drive performance up further.

### Reforms for the masses

Some supporters of these structural reforms seem to think we have finally cracked it. We should convert all schools to academies, with experienced sponsors where there is a history of poor performance. Add in a smattering of free schools to introduce some competition, and there will be no such thing as an underperforming school any more.

But this view depends entirely on a particular definition of under-performance. A floor standard set at 50% does nothing to address the problem of the tail, since even the schools that pass this bar with flying colours still fail the bottom 20%. (And even then, we are assuming that five good GCSEs including English and maths is the standard we should be aiming for, which is a matter of some debate.) The truth is that the structural reforms of the past ten years do not solve this problem. Take London, the highest-performing region in the country,

Figure 12.1 **The small effect of academisation**

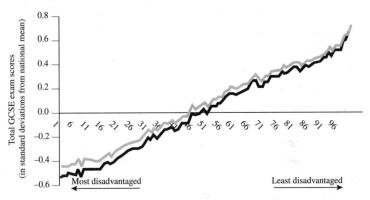

*Pupils' performance at 50% threshold (using all-GCSE performance measure)*

Source: Cook, C. (2012) 'The Social Mobility Challenge for School Reformers', FT Data Blog, 22 February

with more academies than anywhere else. Even here, only five comprehensive schools have over 80% of their pupils getting five good GCSEs including English and maths.

The graph above gives an idea of the effect of setting the floor standard at 50%.[2] The lines represent the cohort of pupils that sat their GCSEs in 2011, ranked in order of how impoverished their neighbourhood is. The black line shows what actually happened: deprivation had a very big impact on performance, with the half of children achieving below the national average being the most deprived half of the cohort. The grey line shows what would happen if you removed all the schools that fall below the 50% floor standard – the 470 or so that we define as underperforming.

This shows that even if you get rid of all of the 'underperforming' schools, the situation is only marginally better: only a few more disadvantaged children perform well. As we have seen earlier in the book, the tail does not consist solely of deprived pupils, but the principle holds. Converting underperforming schools to academies has a positive impact on results, but it can't tackle the tail – because the tail isn't a problem confined to some schools. Almost *every* school fails the tail.

*Can structural reforms help?*
The tail is such an intractable problem precisely because structural reforms like academies, for all their worth, have not solved it. But if the problem is how we are defining underperformance, can we not just change our definition? Well, we have tried. 'Value added' and 'progress' measures are intended to reward schools for doing well with challenging pupils. But what we mean by 'doing well' is just that these pupils perform better than expected given their personal background or prior attainment. That is perhaps a worthy goal, but it does nothing to ensure that the tail actually leave school with a minimum standard of skills, knowledge and qualifications. A new focus on deprived pupils through the 'pupil premium' may yield results, yet it is far from certain whether innovations like the pupil premium can ever be sufficient to overcome the relentless force of the floor standard. And of course this would only help pupils from low-income families, who constitute some, but not all, of the tail.

The problem with trying to drive change using the main accountability system is one of unintended consequences. Experience suggests that we should be sceptical about the feasibility of tweaking performance measures without having adverse effects elsewhere. The most obvious example of this is the floor standard itself. By having a straight cut-off of five grade C GCSEs, schools are driven to focus on those pupils who are on the borderline between grade C and grade D at the expense of higher and lower performers. The performance measures don't recognise or reward the effort of raising a B grade to an A, or an E grade to a D – so the high-fliers and the children who are struggling the most simply matter less to a school than those who sit near an arbitrary line defining satisfactory performance.

Since the main accountability system cannot incentivise schools to focus on the tail, we need to change something for the 20% of pupils who constitute it. The increasing floor standard has raised expectations about what the mainstream of children can achieve, and government has provided incentives for schools to get there. We need to do the same for the tail. Is it possible to create a system that will cater for the tail in the way the main school system doesn't – one with high expectations for the tail's achievement and the incentives to drive schools to fulfil them? Such a system could involve dedicated provision for the tail, or the creation of incentives separate from the main accountability system to encourage existing schools to address the tail.

## Competing for the tail

The existing system successfully drives schools to compete on the performance of 'mainstream' students. What if the children in the tail were given the power to encourage schools to compete for them instead (or as well)? If the mainstream schools system is failing the tail, one option is to give those pupils the opportunity to opt out of their school and go to a different one.

A voucher-style mechanism is the classic device for facilitating this kind of choice. In the basic model, the children in question are given a 'voucher' equivalent to the cost of their education at their current school which they can use to 'buy' a place at a school of their choice. In doing so, they can choose a school that will focus on their needs if their current school is failing to do so, creating an incentive outside of the 'mainstream' system to ensure that these pupils are having their needs met. One such programme, in the District of Columbia in the USA, has achieved a significant improvement in outcomes for the participating children. In Finland, specially commissioned provision ensures that no children are left behind. These very different systems share one key trait: they both provide incentives for schools to focus on those children let down by the traditional system.

## The DC Opportunity Scholarship Programme

In the District of Columbia, poor educational outcomes and low satisfaction with public schools – particularly for pupils from disadvantaged backgrounds – led to the creation of the Opportunity Scholarship Programme in 2004. Lawmakers were particularly concerned with the low rate of high school graduation in DC, which at 60% compares poorly with the national average of 74%. The programme provides scholarships for eligible pupils to attend a private school of their choice. Scholarships are awarded at the level of $8,000, or $12,000 for those in the last four years of compulsory education. This is well under half the average $29,000 spent per pupil in the DC public school system, implying significant potential cost savings.

Between 1,000 and 2,000 children have participated in the programme each year since its inception. Eligibility is determined by the same financial criteria used to identify children eligible to receive free school meals under the Federal Lunch Programme. The vast majority of pupils participating in the scheme are black, with a significant minority of Hispanics, and 92% of enrolled pupils would otherwise be attending a school defined as being 'in need of improvement'. More relevant for the problem of the tail is that the mean reading and maths scores of participating pupils fall around the 30th percentile – higher than the tail of the bottom 20%, but nonetheless suggesting that a significant proportion of participants would be in this cohort.

The programme has yielded a number of positive outcomes.[3] The proportion of students successfully completing high school – the key concern motivating the creation of the programme – was found to be 21 percentage points higher amongst scholarship pupils than for a control group. Reading standards, parental satisfaction and perception of safety have also improved. There was also a discernible competition effect, with 28% of public schools making changes to retain pupils eligible for participation in the programme.

Following the success of the programme, funding has been extended and, for the first time, all students meeting the eligibility criteria will now be able to participate.

*Special education in Finland*

The Finnish school system makes a point of leaving no one behind. While it does not use a voucher mechanism, it does include at its core the idea of dedicated provision for those who are underperforming. In the majority of cases this is provided within the child's current school; a minority are educated at specialist institutions.

In a typical year, around one third of students receive some form of special educational provision in addition to (or instead of) their standard schooling. Most of these children receive part-time special education focused on their specific weaknesses, led by a specialist teacher who works closely with general class teachers to identify underperforming students and address their improvement needs. This approach is flexible and varies from year to year: up to half of children completing compulsory education have had some form of special provision at some point.

Around 8% of children receive full-time special education. For some this takes place at a specialist institution, but many remain in their current school within a dedicated class or stream. It is standard practice, then, for mainstream schools to focus strongly on underperforming pupils and provide them with additional, dedicated support. Since schools are responsible for ensuring that every pupil is ready and able to progress, they have an incentive to focus on underachieving pupils and facilitate specialist provision where they are unable (or unwilling) to cater to these pupils' needs.

The outcome of this approach is high attainment with exceptionally low variation in performance (between and within schools) in comparison with other countries; in other words, the gap is narrowed *and* the bar is raised. The OECD's PISA study shows that Finland has higher performance than most other countries at every level of attainment, and a narrower gap between the top performers and the bottom performers despite pupils at all levels doing better. More pupils perform at a high level and fewer at a low level: the whole attainment spectrum is shifted up compared to other countries. Most importantly, Finnish pupils outperform the OECD average to the greatest extent at the bottom end.

*Giving the tail choice*

These international examples demonstrate the significant improvement in results that can follow from focusing dedicated provision on educating the tail. The government in England could create a system that adapted the best elements of these to the English school system. A voucher-based programme, open to the lowest-performing 20% of children, would create a new system of incentives for schools to focus on these pupils' education and ensure that they receive appropriate specialist provision where mainstream schools are failing to provide the quality of education they require.

A key question in creating such a system would be to determine which children would receive the vouchers: we need to ensure that we are genuinely targeting the tail. Standardised test results at Key Stage 2 (age 11) could be used to determine which children were the lowest-performing 20% across the country; these pupils could be eligible for participation in the programme. Of course, since we know that large gaps in attainment open up very early in children's lives, this kind of programme would arguably benefit primary-age children at least as much as those at secondary level; policy makers should consider whether it is possible to assess children's performance meaningfully at an earlier age in order to identify the 20% most at risk of being failed by the current system.

The experience of the District of Columbia suggests that these vouchers would not necessarily need a funding premium, since the Opportunity Scholarship Programme demonstrates that results can be much improved without additional funding. This may be particularly the case given that many eligible children will also be in receipt of the pupil premium or additional funding for special educational needs.

One controversial aspect of any voucher system is whether pupils should be permitted to use it at non-state schools, thereby 'losing' the money from the state school system. Policy makers could opt to limit the use of vouchers to schools in the state sector. However, the non-state sector in England has significant experience in catering for non-mainstream pupils. Over £1.7 billion of state education funding goes to non-state providers (either charitable or profit-making) each year, since many pupils with SEN opt for specialist, private schools. And, as in Sweden, allowing non-state providers into the system has increased the amount of provision and encouraged specialist schools to develop, as well as having a positive impact on results. The Swedish system does not permit schools to charge a 'top-up' fee in addition to the value of the voucher, thereby removing any concerns over equity of access.

A major result of this kind of reform would be the specialisation of some schools in provision for the pupils in the tail, and the estab-lishment of new schools specialising in catering for those pupils. Just as the free schools programme is now leading to specialist Alterna-tive Provision schools being opened, a change in the admissions code could allow new free schools to be set up that specialise in provision for participants in the tail voucher programme.

But a broader outcome of the reform could be an impact on the main school system itself. Might some mainstream schools choose to specialise in provision for the tail? As we have seen, some schools in Finland are particularly focused on special education and achieve excellent outcomes for those pupils. By creating incentives and pro-viding resources for schools to focus on pupils who need extra help, the Finnish system succeeds in encouraging schools to improve the quality of education for these pupils. Some schools in England now have their own on-site pupil referral units for excluded pupils. Provi-sion for the tail would not have to be segregated in this way, but such developments demonstrate the innovative approaches some schools are taking to cater for pupils who cannot be effectively accommodated within the main system.

Further, the mere possibility of pupils opting out that is provided by a voucher programme could incentivise some schools to focus more on the education of the tail than they do at present. They may, for example, change their deployment of teachers so that the most effective practitioners work with underperforming pupils rather than with the more able, which (as Chris Husbands notes in Chapter 10) is a common issue. This effect may, however, be small in oversubscribed schools whose viability would not be jeopardised by pupils opting out, which is the central reason for creating a mechanism to improve the education of the tail that is separate from the main school system.

## Incentivising results

In welfare-to-work and offender rehabilitation, the government is introducing markets with providers paid on a payment-by-results (PBR) basis to incentivise high-quality work with the most difficult cases. Long-term unemployed individuals are given vocational training, personal skills development, literacy and numeracy education, help with job applications and so on. Repeat offenders are offered similar help, along with housing assistance, family reconciliation or drug or alcohol treatment where necessary. There are two key aspects of PBR. It focuses on outcomes: the providers are held to account for how well they do but are free to choose whatever forms of support or intervention are most appropriate for the individual in question. And there is a very real financial penalty for failure, as providers receive the full value of their contract only if they achieve targets specified by the commissioner, such as the individual staying in work for 12 consecutive months.

These difficult and often intractable cases are clearly analogous to the tail. Pupils in the tail are failed by the mainstream system, which rarely offers provision tailored to their specific needs, and mainstream providers have few, if any, incentives to improve outcomes for these individuals. Could this type of approach be helpful in tackling the tail by incentivising providers both to focus on those pupils and to deliver results? Such a model would be more subtle than a straightforward all-or-nothing voucher system, but its principal benefit would be to provide a mechanism to help those children whose parents are unable or unwilling to exercise choice. The pupil premium is a first step towards this idea, although it focuses on a somewhat different cohort and, importantly, its payment is not contingent on outcomes (although Chris Paterson considers this question in Chapter 6, and Tim Leunig and Gill Wyness do so in Chapter 3). Examples from other, more developed sectors may prove more instructive.

*Payment-by-results in action*
In Peterborough, the private and third sectors have come together to take a new approach to rehabilitating offenders. Sodexo, the private company that runs Peterborough Prison, came together in March 2010 with St Giles Trust, a charity, to run a PBR pilot to reduce the rate of reoffending. The organisations work together to provide specialised, intensive support to offenders leaving the prison, to maximise their likelihood of finding housing and employment (factors shown to significantly impact upon reoffending rates). The pilot will see dedicated support provided to 3,000 short-term prisoners over a six-year period.

The pilot is funded through a social impact bond, in which private investors provide the capital (up to £5 million) and, crucially, assume the financial risk. The investors' return operates on a PBR basis: the more successful the programme, the greater the return. Payments are made only if the intervention reduces reoffending rates by at least 7.5 percentage points, and greater drops in reoffending yield commensurately greater returns. Since the return to investors is funded out of the savings to government resulting from reduced reoffending, there is no additional cost to the taxpayer; indeed, there should be a long-term net benefit, assuming that the savings can be realised. If the programme is unsuccessful and the required performance threshold is not reached, the investors receive no return on their money.

In the first appraisal of the scheme, HM Chief Inspector of Prisons described the pilot as 'promising' and said it 'provided the best reintegration support we have seen in a local prison'.

*Changing schools' incentives*
How could such a system work if applied to the education of the tail? As with a simple voucher system, eligibility could be determined by

existing standardised tests, with secondary school provision for the lowest-performing 20% of children at Key Stage 2 commissioned on a PBR basis.

The design of the funding model and its financial penalties is a key consideration. Doncaster Prison has been privately operated by Serco since its establishment in 1994. The contract renewal in 2011 introduced a PBR element for the first time to encourage more effective rehabilitation of prisoners. Under the terms of the contract, 10% of the contract value (a total of £25 million over the life of the contract) is conditional on the prison reducing by 5 percentage points the proportion of prisoners who reoffend within a year of release. A similar system in an educational context might offer a financial incentive for increasing the proportion of that provider's cohort who performed above a specified level. For example, a provider might have to increase the number of children who achieved better than expected progress on the government's measure, or the number who achieved the national benchmark of five good GCSEs, or the number who attained the national average performance. The choice of measure would depend on the level of expectations of the commissioner, so there is every reason to think high – and for this reason commissioners should be wary of value-added or progress-based measures that may limit the absolute attainment of the pupils in the tail. Of course, measures that were harder to achieve would come with a commensurately larger incentive.

An alternative to a simple threshold would be a system with a 'sliding scale'. The Work Programme, the government's new PBR welfare-to-work scheme, operates on this basis, with providers paid according to how challenging the case is. The maximum fee for each client ranges from £4,050 for a jobseeker's allowance claimant aged 18–24 to £13,120 for a former incapacity benefit claimant not considered immediately ready for work. A similar system could be devised in an educational context, perhaps taking into account criteria such as the level of previous attainment, special educational needs or deprivation (although the latter two are already addressed by the funding system). Obliging providers to accept any eligible child (or to select them at random if there were capacity constraints) would negate the danger of 'cherry picking', where providers select the easier cases in order to maximise their return.

The most important factor determining the success of this kind of reform is the choice of commissioner. If the commissioner's incentives are not aligned with the needs of the child, or if the commissioner has insufficient capacity or capability, a PBR-based system will fail to achieve its full potential.

As in a classic voucher-style system, the parent could act as the commissioner, choosing the school they felt was best for their child. However, some parents will not or cannot fulfil this role, and given the complexities of PBR commissioning, it is unlikely that many parents would be suitably equipped for this. Central government – or one of its organs, such as the Education Funding Agency or the Children's or Schools Commissioners – could take on this responsibility. But it is questionable whether this is best done at a national level, given that centrally based commissioners are unlikely to have a detailed knowledge of local provision across the country.

Local authorities could perform the function, as they currently do for some vulnerable children such as those in care. In the Finnish system, local authorities are responsible for ensuring that children receive appropriate special education provision, whether within their existing school or at an alternative institution. A further option would be for a pupil's existing school to commission from another provider, if the school itself was unable or unwilling to deliver a suitable education for that pupil. Under this model, which is being piloted in England for provision for excluded pupils, the commissioning school would continue to be held accountable for the pupil's outcomes, incentivising the school to ensure that the commissioned provision was effective. If all schools were held to account for the performance of the tail – by government or by parents – they would have a strong incentive to commission effective provision on a PBR basis if they were unable to effectively educate their pupils in the tail. Knowing the pupils in question, the commissioning schools would be in a position to structure performance objectives appropriately to maximise the efficacy of a PBR approach.

## Incentives to give them a chance

While there are lots of enlightening examples – of vouchers, of dedicated provision, of payment-by-results – the models proposed here are untried and untested in the context of the English school system. But there seems scant argument against trying them. As the District of Columbia's voucher programme and Peterborough Prison's social impact bond show, they can come at no additional cost to the system. Certainly, these approaches are in keeping with the current government's philosophies around choice and accountability in public services. And, above all, they would apply to children who are currently leaving the system with nothing. They can't make things worse, so perhaps it's time that policy makers gave those children a system of their own, with incentives that would give them a chance.

# 13

# Behaviour and the tail

*Charlie Taylor*

Every teacher has their own version of the dream. As the summer holidays come to an end, the thought of returning to school begins to enter the teacher's relaxed consciousness. At 4 am they wake in a cold sweat, they are back in the classroom and the children are out of control. The details vary, but the theme remains the same, teachers' greatest, primeval fear is played out in a series of scenes where the children run wild and there is nothing we can do to stop them.

Deep down we teachers all have a fear of losing control of our pupils, and when it happens, it is a horrible experience. A head teacher colleague once begged me to come and help him with a pupil he couldn't control. I was taken to the school library where, cornered like a stag at bay, by the school keeper and two teaching assistants, a minute, underfed-looking 6-year-old was pacing up and down trying to look menacing. So big and powerful had this child become in the collective consciousness of the school that the staff had forgotten to get the basics of behaviour right – be clear about what you expect and stick to your guns. The more the school backed off, the more unsafe the child felt (despite appearances to the contrary, 6-year-olds don't like being in control) and the worse his behaviour had become.

Keeping control of most schoolchildren is generally reasonably simple. When teachers are firm, clear and consistent and build good relationships, most children will behave well most of the time, particularly if the school has well-organised systems to back teachers up.

There is, however, a group of children who need more than this. They usually come from chaotic homes where education is not particularly valued and their parents are unable for all sorts of reasons to control their children. Often a little digging into these children's backgrounds will reveal an extra factor that seems to have tipped a child into more extreme behaviour. Many of these children have been recently bereaved, have witnessed domestic violence or have parents who have health problems (mental, physical or both). Often there has been trauma in the child's early life or for some reason the child has failed to form an early attachment to an adult.

The behaviour of these children can be awful. They are unable to get the sort of emotional fulfilment that most children get from behaving well, so they move into a negative, destructive pattern that leads to them becoming so difficult that either their school gets rid of them or they simply stop turning up.

They often end up in pupil referral units or other sorts of alternative provision. If they are lucky, they go to a place which helps them to overcome their difficulties and prepares them for the next stage of their lives. However, for many, exclusion is the beginning of a spiral into crime, drugs, alcohol, anti-social behaviour, dysfunctional family and social life, and prison. Some 85% of children in young offenders' institutions have spent a period of their education in alternative provision.

This is a group of children whose behaviour or distress is beyond that which most schools feel they can reasonably cope with. They put enormous strain on the school. They disrupt the learning of themselves and others, they exhaust their teachers and they take up disproportionate amounts of the senior teachers' time dealing with them and with complaints about them. Other children express distress in less overt ways, such as becoming withdrawn, beginning to self-harm or developing eating disorders. Many of these children may be suffering from mental health difficulties that are causing or contributing to their behaviour. Mental health services for children are generally provided by local CAMHS (Child and Adolescent Mental Health Services). There is enormous frustration in schools about the way that CAMHS often operate, both in the organisation of services and the quality of help that children receive.

## Mental health services

When staff at a school become concerned about the mental health of a pupil they will want to get specialist help from CAMHS. However, local rules often don't allow them to make direct referrals even when the parent is asking for help. Instead they have to persuade the parent to visit their GP and get a referral. Assuming the parent gets round to visiting the doctor, and the GP agrees, then the referral will arrive at CAMHS. GPs hear only the parent's version of the problem and they will rarely seek the views of the school. It can then take months before the parent is given an appointment, or they may be offered a more prompt initial assessment, but there can then be a long wait before any treatment is offered.

A proportion of referrals are rejected because they are seen as 'inappropriate' or because the child does not have a diagnosable condition. The reasons for rejection are not shared with schools because of patient confidentiality, and schools even report that children are rejected because they are 'too severe'.

Inevitably many of the parents whose children are referred to CAMHS lead chaotic lives. They often live in the present and if things on the day of the appointment are OK at home then they may well not turn up. When these disorganised families miss two appointments they are removed from the list. Parents can have complicated and time-consuming journeys to get to CAMHS clinics and this is another cause of high 'did not attend' (DNA) rates. Some families are put off by the stigma they associate with the words 'mental health'. Even if they get through the door to begin treatment, they are already reluctant patients and often if they don't like what they are offered, or the therapist changes, they just stop coming. There is no requirement for services to publish data on attendance, though a few do, so it is not possible to compare DNA rates between different areas, and find out why some may be so much better than others.

This remoteness between clinicians and the communities they serve means the levels of engagement are often patchy. Despite this, clinicians are often reluctant to take their work into schools. There are, of course, some children who need to be seen away from school because of the nature of their difficulties, but if services were available in schools teachers or staff could ensure that children attended appointments and could have ongoing dialogue with clinicians about open cases and new referrals.

This simple change has proved extremely difficult for head teachers or local authority officers to achieve. There is huge resistance to any change in the way CAMHS operates, and at times it seems to be constituted for the convenience of the workers rather than their patients. Important decisions are made about the lives of these children, yet the professionals in schools, who know them best, who work with them every day and who will most acutely feel the consequences of these decisions, have little or no input into the process. Where services are located in schools they report, inevitably, better attendance.

This inflexibility within services means that many children do not get treatment. These tend to come from the poorest households with chaotic families who lack the motivation or know-how to make the system work. At my school First Steps is a unit for children who have been thrown out of mainstream nurseries. When children are three years old there is an opportunity to change things before the child and the parents have got into established patterns of behaviour. All the children who come to First Steps have speech, language and communication disorder, and they have all been referred to and then thrown out of NHS speech therapy groups. We know that prisoners are more likely to have communication difficulties than the general population. So we can make a reasonable assumption that not being able to communicate properly makes people more likely to offend. It would make sense to address this as soon as possible after it has been identified. I contacted my local NHS Speech Therapy service and suggested that they ran a group in First Steps. They could do the therapy and my staff would do the behaviour.

'But Charlie,' came the astonishing reply, 'we're a clinic-based service.'

Schools complain that they are not kept informed about the progress of treatment from CAMHS workers. Often patient confidentiality is used as a reason for not sharing the most basic information, such as whether the pupil is turning up for appointments. It can be almost impossible to find out if the treatment is helping the child or making any difference. Schools do not, of course, want to know the details of therapy sessions, but they do want to know that their pupils are getting the help they need, because if not, then they need to think again. CAMHS can divest themselves of responsibility for a child simply by striking them off when they don't attend. This is not a luxury afforded to schools, which have to keep going with very challenging, disruptive or distressed children day after day. There often seems to be a lack of understanding in CAMHS about what this experience is like for teachers.

Schools and teachers get little training in helping children with mental health difficulties and often they don't realise that good education promotes good mental health. They sometimes expect a blue light service from CAMHS when a child is in difficulties, not realising that the simple school virtues of being organised, predictable, calm, setting clear boundaries, being understanding and kind are often enough to get children through difficult times. However, too often there is a gulf between schools and CAMHS and the communication can be appalling.

As part of the assessment, schools are asked to fill out a quick psychological questionnaire about the child. This is often the only information that the school is asked for and many schools say they are never contacted by phone, let alone visited.

## Conduct disorders and medication

Often, the first schools know about one of their pupils attending
CAMHS is when the parent tells the class teacher or tutor that the
child has a diagnosis of a disorder or condition. There is a bewil-
dering range of conditions that are diagnosed, including attention
deficit hyperactivity disorder (ADHD), oppositional defiance disorder
(ODD), attention deficit disorder (ADD), semantic pragmatic disorder, autistic spectrum disorder (ASD), depression, anxiety, eating disorder, obsessive compulsive disorder (OCD). There continues to be an
increase both in the range and the amount of diagnosis. Many psychiatrists say there is under-diagnosis of conditions such as ADHD in this
country, yet much of the process of diagnosis seems to be piecemeal
and flawed. One of the important factors in the diagnosis of ADHD
is that the behaviour associated with it is seen in a range of different
contexts. You can't have the condition if you only show the symptoms at home. The NICE guidelines on diagnosing ADHD encourage
doctors to get evidence from more sources than just the parent and
the child at consultation, but this isn't mandatory. There is some rare
good practice where before they diagnose, doctors observe the child
in school and talk to the teachers, but usually, beyond the subjective
questionnaires, schools are not consulted. Teachers are amazed and
aghast when particular pupils receive a diagnosis of ADHD. The child
is fine in school, but the parent has managed to convince a paediatrician in a five-minute consultation that the behaviour of their child is
not due to their abilities as a parent but to some pathological defect
in the child's brain.

Many children who receive a diagnosis are prescribed a psychotropic drug to treat their condition. These drugs, commonly known as
Ritalin, are forms of amphetamine not materially different from the
recreational, Class B drug, speed. Indeed, one of the risks of prescribing Ritalin is that the drug is used or sold by other family members.
Ritalin is a powerful drug with some concerning side effects, yet it
can be prescribed for years as the result of a five-minute consultation.

Many children who take it fail to grow properly and, because of the stimulant effect, they often have difficulty sleeping at night. This then leads to the prescription of a sleeping drug to counter the effects of the stimulant. Some worrying research into the effects of these drugs on children, such as the Raine study in Western Australia,[1] suggests that the ADHD medication has little or no impact on the child's ability to succeed in school in the long term. There is also a concern that as they grow up, children will feel that there is a medical solution to any problem that comes along and they may be more tempted to self-medicate on drugs and alcohol.

For parents who are desperate for help, getting medication seems like a simple solution. The parent receives confirmation that the child's behaviour is not their fault or responsibility, but due to a problem in the child's brain. The child is put on medication that is likely to calm them down, at least in the short to medium term. This collusion to diagnose is further compounded by the possibility that the parent may be able to collect Disabled Living Allowance (DLA) for their child. DLA is given to parents to help them with the cost of looking after a disabled child. The way it is spent is not monitored, but it could be used for the extra cost of taking a child to lots of appointments, for modifying the home or for child-care costs. The level of DLA parents receive is the result of an assessment of their needs. Parents who have a child with a diagnosis of ADHD have the right to apply for DLA and many are successful, though it is not possible to get accurate figures. The parent has to fill out a form in which they make a case for receiving DLA. Schools are asked to endorse DLA applications and write a letter in support of the parent. Parents can be persuasive and even aggressive in their attempts to get schools to sign off DLA forms. Where word has got around and where doctors are ready diagnosers and prescribers, schools receive waves of these applications. This is not surprising, there is money at stake. The average allowance paid for DLA is £40 a week, but it can go up to £120. DLA is a supplementary payment, so it doesn't reduce any other benefits that are being paid to parents. Some parents from poor backgrounds readily seek the

ADHD diagnosis. Head teachers describe parents encouraging children to misbehave at school or when they go to the doctor, and there are even stories of parents giving their children sugary drinks or Red Bull before an appointment with the paediatrician.

Psychotropic drugs do not treat the condition, they just mask the symptoms. For schools there is a temptation to push for a child to be on medication, as this may make them easier to handle. When I started at my school we gave one boy his dose of Ritalin every morning because his mother was too disorganised to manage herself. At lunchtime the drug would wear off and he would become agitated and sometimes violent until he received a top-up tablet at 2 pm, after which he would calm down. What was the real child? What was the real behaviour? The drugged-up, apathetic half-zombie he became when the drug kicked in or the distressed little boy we saw for what we called his witching hour, between 1 and 2 pm every afternoon. His home life was unimaginably awful, he shouldn't have been living with his mother, but to social workers he presented as docile and compliant. The drugs allowed us and other professionals off the hook.

The use of medication to treat children with conduct disorders has increased exponentially. However, we have some way to go before we reach the levels seen in America, where 12% of children are on a psychotropic drug such as Ritalin at any one time and 40% of children spend a period on medication. American children swallow 8½ tonnes of Ritalin or its equivalents every year.

There is a common perception among mental health workers that up to one in three children of school age has a diagnosable condition and another one in three is on the borderline. If this is to be believed then there are six of these children in each classroom in the country. There is a risk here that medicine begins to encroach on to what is really education's turf. Ask most teachers and, apart from schools in the most challenging catchment areas, they will probably feel this is a wild exaggeration.

There is a case for saying that behaviour in our schools has never been better, not so much because the children have necessarily improved, but because teachers have got better at dealing with it and some of the damaging laissez-faire philosophies of managing behaviour have been abandoned in favour of tighter regimes. There is a greater understanding among teachers that children who are rarely challenged by their parents will need very clear boundaries if they are to succeed at school. There is a real concern that what was once considered normal behaviour for children, such as boisterousness or even shyness, is now becoming a diagnosable condition.

Teachers, when confronted by a child who is loud or disruptive, know what to do. They usually have the confidence and experience to handle the behaviour and help the child back on to the straight and narrow. Once a child has the diagnosis of a mental health disorder then teachers feel out of their depth and stop using tried-and-tested methods. The common-sense response of the teacher no longer feels like enough to cope with a problem they don't understand. Teachers are rarely trained in working with children with ADHD, so they are given the problem to solve, without being given any solution.

## A joined-up approach

There are some exceptional examples of CAMHS that are able to help children, families and their schools to create a joined-up approach to improving behaviour. Neil Dawson and Brenda McHugh from the Marlborough Education Unit in Westminster see their relationships with schools as a crucial part of helping children to change. They are not driven to, nor do they seek, diagnosis. Rather their role is to work with children and directly with their parents in order to help them to understand and break down the patterns that have resulted in the child's poor behaviour. This is a pragmatic approach: the parent and child receive therapeutic input, but there is also an emphasis on giving the parent the practical skills to stay calm and in control. Children attend the unit with their parents for up to six months. Much of the work is centred around parents, in groups, helping each other.

Those who are successful, and whose child is about to leave, give advice and support to newer families. The staff at the Marlborough realise that it is essential that schools are part of the solution. They work closely with teachers to make sure they know what the child is trying to achieve and what progress is being made in school. Regular training is available to school staff so they understand both where the behaviour is coming from and, most importantly, how they can help the child to change. Rather than hiding behind confidentiality, the Marlborough is committed to sharing as much information as is possible and necessary. The unit also places workers in schools to help run groups for parents whose children are at risk of descending into more serious behaviour difficulties. This type of partnership arrangement between schools and CAMHS is all too rare and must become the norm if the behaviour and mental health of the most difficult children is to improve.

In Lincolnshire, every school and college in the county has a linked Primary Mental Health Worker who provides free telephone advice and face-to-face consultation when there are concerns about a child's mental health. They can accept direct referrals to CAMHS, deliver mental health therapies in school, run groups for children and provide free training and support on mental health issues. This means that there is less risk of missed appointments, because parents often do not have to take their children across town for therapy.

In Worcestershire prescribing of medication for ADHD is beginning to fall because teachers and educational psychologists are involved with doctors in the process of diagnosis. Psychological interventions are usually recommended to begin with and medication is only prescribed after consultation and in the most serious cases.

This sort of approach needs to be adopted nationally to reduce the reliance on powerful and potentially dangerous drugs to mask the symptoms of children's distress. If a child is prescribed drugs for the condition, parents should have a thorough explanation of the implications of the treatment, including the side effects in the short and long term. Medication should be just a part of a treatment programme that seeks to modify the behaviour and understand its causes. The use of medication should be time-limited and reviewed thoroughly and regularly. This joined-up approach to treatment should also apply to DLA, which should only be granted for most mental health conditions in exceptional circumstances.

The current system of remote diagnosis and treatment should end. Extending the range of conditions and disorders that psychiatrists are able to describe and diagnose will not make children any better. CAMHS workers must roll up their sleeves, abandon the comfort of the clinic and work locally in schools and homes.

CAMHS should be held to account for the impact they have on the lives of children. These should include real measures, not just subjective surveys. Did the child behave better at school? Did their attendance get better? Did their achievements at school improve? Treatment needs to result in children being able to lead more successful lives. The attendance rates at clinics should be published and this should include data on children from poor families and other vulnerable groups. This level of accountability is no more than is expected of schools. Providers of mental health services who fail across a range of these and clinical measures should be expected to improve or go out of business. Schools need to do more than just moan about their local CAMHS, they should be represented on the new health and well-being boards and on local government bodies who are commissioning services, where their concerns will be heard and addressed.

More mental health professionals should be working in schools so that children and families are offered a more joined-up approach to getting help. Mental health treatment can become part of a support system for children who are in difficulties, without a relentless reliance on diagnosis and medication. The focus should be on changing damaging patterns of behaviour, not simply reacting to symptoms. Ultimately, on the most practical level, if CAMHS support is not helping children to become more settled in school, easier to teach and therefore more likely to succeed academically and socially, it is simply not effective. It cannot continue to operate in a clinical bubble.

The problems of delivering effective mental health services to children do not come down simply to resources, as workers always believe. Of course more money would be welcome, but the problems will be solved by changes in structure that will lead to changes in ways of working and culture, which will in turn lead to children and families getting the help they need.

# 14

# Crime and the tail

*Danny Kruger*

## Introduction

In this essay I suggest the creation of 'Civil Zones' in neighbourhoods affected by poverty and crime, defined areas where the community works together to shape the culture of young people towards college, work and family stability.

Schools should be the institutional centrepiece of Civil Zones, the site, both symbolic and real, of the community's commitment to positive childhood. Yet schools are not the whole answer. We need a diversity of institutions for young people to belong to, shape, and bounce between.

Civil Zones would be distinguished by the deliberate attempt to build the social capital, the institutional and relational strength of a community, so that the most powerful agency of all – the culture of the neighbourhood – supports pro-social norms.

## The relational view

Research beyond the frontier of the brain has empirically confirmed the 'attachment' theory developed by John Bowlby in the 1950s, which proposed that our behaviour is conditioned by our experience of love, or its absence, from our primary caregiver.[1]

We increasingly understand how the brain develops not of its own accord – by some individualist growth gene – but through relationships; pathways in the brain are literally laid down in response to our interactions with and experience of others. Uniquely among mammals, newborn human babies are neurologically nearly blank, with only the most basic capabilities; most brain development is done outside the womb.

The great project of a child's development is the laying down of a million tracks between the amygdala (the primitive, fight-or-flight-oriented 'dog brain') and the pre-frontal cortex (or 'human brain', which does the thinking). Rationalising our emotions is the business of adulthood, and this function is acquired through effective support on the journey of adolescence.

The people around us – from our mothers onwards – explain the world to us. These relational circumstances, not our innate abilities or disabilities, are our real inheritance, our real ticket in the lottery of life.

Leon Feinstein's research, cited in Chapter 1, into the 1970 cohort showed how social and economic status can matter more, in terms of academic and professional success, than ability; dim rich kids do better at school, and in life, than bright poor ones. Importantly, it's not the money that matters but the networks and culture that rich and poor inhabit: studies into educational failure show that the state of a child's neighbourhood makes more of a difference than the poverty of his or her own family.[2]

Mark Granovetter's famous work into social networks showed how a poor community might be rich in 'strong ties', the relationships of family and neighbours, but lack the 'weak ties' which give professional people access to ideas and opportunities for success.[3]

## Crime

The relational view accounts for the connectedness of what have become known as 'multiple needs', or the 'trouble' in 'troubled families'. And these needs, this trouble, are concentrated in the essential relational breach we call crime.

Crime is the great proxy, the catch-all for every kind of social breakdown; cause and consequence of family dysfunction, mental ill health, bad education, poor housing, unemployment, addiction and poverty. One might say it's where these problems go to unwind and express themselves: the context in which they are most confident.

Traditionally, crime was seen as an individual phenomenon. The great Victorian reformers, appalled at the messy squalor of Georgian gaols, designed prisons on the basis of personal sin and expiation: rows of individual cells, light and hygienic, in which prisoners could reflect on their own wrongdoing. Community, except in the controlled environment of the church or chapel, was designed out; imprisonment was the experience of being alone.

This individualist philosophy underlies our criminal justice system. The courts, rightly, take no account of one's relationships in their consideration of guilt or innocence; our legal system rests on the assumption of personal responsibility.[4]

Yet there is surely a need to consider association and relationships in understanding the causes of crime, and deciding what to do with criminals. Crime, or desistance from crime, represents a nuanced conversation between 'criminogenic needs' and 'criminal propensity', between external circumstances and inner disposition. All experience (not to mention the founding ethics of our culture) shows how weak our moral disposition is, when removed from what Professor Per-Olaf Wikström of Cambridge calls the 'moral context', the 'informal social controls' in which young people make their decisions; how completely lightless we are without the stars of our community to navigate by.[5]

Crime can be seen as an expression of individual sinfulness, and so it is; but a more useful view is to see it as the evidence of a relational deficit, a curtailing of the chain of loyalties which should link our self-concern, through local patriotism, to a general empathy.

Attachment to our family and local community should transmit commitment to the wider society. But if the first attachments are somehow dysfunctional, the transmission fails to happen; what should be a nation at peace becomes a war of tribes; and what should be an empathic concern for others becomes a clear division between us and them, 'my people' and 'others'.

## A social solution

What is the right response to dysfunctional communities? My answer is that social problems need social solutions. Communities have within themselves the assets – the wealth of experience and relation-ship, the aspirations and know-how – necessary for well-being. The economist Hernando de Soto has detailed the 'dead capital' in devel-oping countries (unregistered assets which have a far greater latent value than the sum of foreign aid); similarly, we might argue that there is more latent social capital in poor communities than all the money and 'services' government could inject.[6]

Government should stop thinking of itself as a repairman with a job to deploy expensive tools, spare parts and expertise to 'fix' 'broken' communities. Instead, the task for all of us is to nurture, channel, or unleash (natural metaphors being preferable to mechanical ones) the capabilities that exist in society already.

Put another way, policy making and social theory needs to adopt an 'asset-based' (or 'strength-based') rather than a 'deficit' model of action, one focused on what an individual or community already has, rather than on what they lack.

This is in some ways a tough call: strengths do not 'present', as social workers say, as obviously and insistently as deficits, and drawing out an individual's strength requires more than a referral to the appropriate universal service. Indeed, the 'presenting' – often crit-ical – issue usually needs most immediate attention: but only to clear the way to the real challenge of maximising strengths.

So, for example, a rough sleeper's principal feature – what we should attend to most assiduously – is not his lack of a home, or the offence of begging, or his precise mental health diagnosis, but his love of the countryside, or his skill with computers, or his passion for helping others. Certainly, he needs a roof over his head, tonight if possible; but by reinforcing these positives we build up a social asset – and make it more likely that the right remedy for the deficit will be taken, and be successful.

This is not to say that we should be indifferent to problems. Indeed, a strength-based approach should include an explicit focus on a particular indicator of success or failure: crime levels.

But we fall into the mistake of the 'deficit' model if we pursue crime reduction, and its attendant dysfunctions, head-on. As Maruna and LeBel have argued, both the traditional responses to crime – punishment and welfare, carrot and stick – are merely variations on a theme, which is to look at the individual through the prism of his problems.[7]

As Jonathan Sachs has argued in another context, *shalom* – 'peace' – is not merely the absence of war, but a positive experience of right relationships. This is difficult to capture in the abstract – we are better at identifying bad citizenship than good – but you know it when you see it. Peace means all the flourishing which well-governed, well-cultured communities are capable of.[8]

For war, read crime; for peace, read civilisation, the institutions and habits of a good society. Crime and civilisation are opposing forces, locked in conflict; as one advances, the other retreats.[9]

The advance of civilisation will be through the maximisation of society's strengths: more people, more organisations, fulfilling their potential, widening their spheres of positive influence, germinating and multiplying their good effects.

To adapt a topical argument, we certainly need social deficit reduction, but most of all we need social growth.

The source and structure of 'social growth' is institutions: the voluntary combination of individuals in communal arrangements which mediate reciprocal obligations. The decline of institutional life in the West has a direct link to rising crime; an anti-crime strategy should explicitly seek to nurture the growth of social institutions.[10]

This holds out the prospect of a major alteration in the role and position of the state. Rather than being the principal agent, and centre-stage, in the lives of local communities, the combined officials of government should give way to a 'social sector' of private, voluntary agencies, and themselves occupy the backstage role of commissioning and standard-setting, explicitly tasked to strengthen the social sector and, where possible, work through it.

Private agencies, thereby, could move from a purely reactive role to one which includes the long-term preventative work they have always aspired to do, but which the systems and imperatives of a politicised bureaucracy have always frustrated.

**Total school**

I have argued that society has natural strengths, which – rather than its weaknesses or deficits – should be the object of our efforts; that crime is the great proxy which enables us to measure the strength or weakness of a community; that this strength or weakness is the presence or absence of healthy family and social relationships.

Relationships are supported by institutions – artificial and formal, but human-shaped and conducive to safe and productive social life.

With such breakdown all around, and the lack of any structure or authority in children's lives, it is natural to build up the school as the principal source of moral and practical authority in our communities. We know that a good school can turn around the life of a child apparently destined by family background to a dysfunctional future; we know that good education cuts crime, irrespective of a young person's economic circumstances.[11]

It is tempting to believe, therefore, that the answer lies in 'total school': the extension of school to become a sort of megahub, open

16 hours a day and at weekends, delivering family services and child care, responsible for a wrap-around holistic support for the child.

But I worry that the 'total school' philosophy – we might call it 'schoolism' – is a new version of the founding fault of secondary education: the attempt to contain young people rather than release them.

Secondary education was an uncomfortable afterthought, a patch-up job as industrialisation, overpopulation and humane legislation ended the millennia-old practice of boys and girls joining the productive economy as they passed puberty. Now we had millions of super-numerary teenagers, and a strange new stage of life called adolescence. No one knew what to do with them, or it.[12]

So we simply extended to adolescents the model of provision offered to pre-pubescents. Passive learning, treating young people like receptacles ('education is a drawing out, not a putting in', as Jeeves suggested to Gussie Fink-Nottle on the occasion of the prize-giving speech); long hours sitting in rows; and the expectation that teenagers will take orders with the same pliant willingness, the same 'adult-knows-best' attitude of an 8-year old.

It is little wonder that we struggle to manage secondary school classrooms, and that teenagers are regarded as liabilities – liable to lash out and kill us – to be sat upon or humoured for the few years it takes them to rejoin the human race. I exaggerate, but this is arguable: secondary schools are warehouses for our young people, vast teencare centres where the unhappy inmates are drilled or entertained for six or eight hours a day so the rest of us can go about our business unmolested.

## How it could be

By this, somewhat parodic, view schools in some of the most deprived areas resemble a mix between a Forward Operating Base in Helmand province – a safe haven in enemy territory – and the Guantanamo Bay prison, a dump for dangerous people we don't know what to do with. This is a tragedy, and a sin not just of commission (a generation of bored and anti-social children) but of omission: the waste of what might have been.

As we are starting to learn from neuroscience – and as we already knew from every literary tradition in the world, all of which have the quest fable – adolescence is in fact a highly creative and exciting time. It is the time for intellectual and physical adventure, for pioneering alone and in small bands of peers, for 'big muscle movements' as John Abbott says, for ideological iconoclasm, creativity and self-definition.[13] It is when pious children become atheists for a time, or the other way around; when brave young men and women set out to circumnavigate their worlds, to return – one hopes – with a deeper, better, updated commitment to home. It is the time for liberalism, precursor and preparer of the deeper, better conservatism to come in maturity.

What are the conditions of that healthy adolescence? We have to find a model of education that honours adolescence rather than represses it. We need a far more creative approach to learning which is not bound to a classroom – but which, when it is, makes kids kings and queens of infinite space, so inspiring is it to learn about our world.

I am not sure this vision of adolescence can be delivered by a single institution, a local monolith which young people are legally obliged to attend, and have no or minimal power to influence or change.

Rather than 'total school', a child, no less than a neighbourhood itself, needs a diversity of institutions. Children, no less than adults, need a vibrant third space between work (or school) and home; the place of voluntary association which is neither economic/educational (daytime) nor domestic (night-time), but social (evening). This period, of course, between school and bed, is when most youth crime is committed.

The place of the youth club has long been derided and down-graded, partly through the fault of the youth clubs themselves, but there has never been a greater need for a thriving youth sector to complement the role of schools and families. As Wilkie and his co-authors argue, good youth work does what parents and schools on their own cannot: it nurtures the moral character of young people and escorts them as they travel, willingly if erratically, into adulthood.[14]

## Civil Zones

To recap: poor communities have latent social capital, and our focus should be to grow this capital through strengthening the institutions which provide authority and positive relationships. Civilisation is composed of these institutions, and the habits they engender; crime, which is the proxy of other social problems, is in conflict with civilisation, one retreating as the other advances. The advance of civilisation will be through the growth, in numbers and strength, of positive social institutions, not least schools and youth centres.

Here, then, is a big simple idea to help civilisation grow and strengthen in poor communities which are affected by crime. 'Civil Zones' will be areas where the community, and public agencies, deliberately work together on a 'strength-based' strategy for crime reduction, which focuses not on crime but on the talents and assets of local people, including but not confined to those at risk of involvement in crime.

The Civil Zone idea is inspired by the example and experience of the Harlem Children's Zone (HCZ) in New York City. HCZ is ten years through a 20-year project whose specific mission is to achieve a cultural tipping-point, when it becomes the social norm for children to assume they are going to college rather than to prison.

The idea is that interventions on their own are of limited value: what matters is the culture of the community, which interventions might or might not affect, positively or negatively; hence the decision to concentrate on a tightly defined geographical area.

Harlem Children's Zone has a range of highly ambitious and straightforward interventions, from 'spotters' employed to find pregnant girls in the streets and persuade them to engage in HCZ's ante-natal support, through HCZ's Pre-K and Kindergarten, to HCZ's own charter schools and, finally, mentoring and support for the project's successes: Harlem students at colleges all over the USA.

The project has already received highly favourable attention – including the commitment by President Obama to create dozens of 'Promise Neighborhoods' across the USA, modelled on the HCZ. Although final evaluation must wait for ten more years, there is reason to be hopeful that this project will achieve its aim of changing the culture of one of the poorest parts of North America.

HCZ is beginning to get attention in the UK too. Michael Gove, the education secretary, visited it in 2011, and in 2012 Save the Children published a report calling for 'English Children's Zones' to be established, a policy which the authors describe as 'simple in purpose and great in ambition'.[15] They argue that the value of Children's Zones is that they are 'doubly holistic', meaning they connect schools to the community, and that they follow the child through time. Zones overcome both the silo mentality and the short-termism of the traditional public sector.

As the Save the Children report makes clear, there are important ways in which the HCZ model should be altered for use in England. The HCZ is a single organisation, albeit one providing a multitude of services. Instead, we need a diversity of local institutions. As Save the Children says, schools are important, but they are not lead contributors. Leadership should be vested in a network of community organisations, and crucially, in individual local leaders who emerge as the champions of the community.

The explicit focus should be on identifying and cultivating the institutional assets of the community, supporting the local churches and charities, the small businesses and neighbourhood groups to become what they already, perhaps latently, are: hubs of street democracy, sources of informal support and conduits of social authority.

What do institutions like these need in order to fulfil this natural function? A purpose, and some power. The government is already taking great strides to localise budgets and decision making to groups

of citizens who demonstrate the appetite and aptitude for local responsibility. The task for Civil Zones is to win, and then to distribute
among the neighbourhood, money and power from central and local
government over welfare and training, housing, public health and
education, and if not criminal justice itself, some of the management
of probation and community punishments. All these services have a
direct impact on behaviour and, therefore, on the local moral environment; within tight bounds, they should be managed or influenced by
the community they affect.

Civil Zones should be established to maximise the strength of the
community. But the target for achievement should be the reduction of
a negative: crime.

This clear, measurable proxy enables the responsible use of public
money. Civil Zones are a natural fit for Social Impact Bonds, by which
private investors fund a programme with clear outcome targets which,
when met, trigger a payment by the state. The taxpayer is thereby
'de-risked'; the government is buying results, not financing failure.
Investors are repaid – perhaps with interest to cover their assumption
of risk – in the event of success, enabling them to capitalise new programmes or extend existing ones.

## Postscript: the politics

The columnist and campaigner Sir Simon Jenkins recently said he
wouldn't go to any more drugs conferences because 'all they talk
about is drugs'. The real challenge, he said, is politics. Why don't
good ideas get implemented? Why do obstacles that everyone sees
not get removed? Why is the public sector so short-term, bureaucratic
and ineffective?

There is a danger that all we're talking about is education, or crime
policy, when we need to talk about politics.

In the end, change in Britain will come about because of a political
shift amounting, in scale and significance, to constitutional change

– albeit with the key factor as the culture of the country rather than the structure of politics. When citizens have the will, and the power, to manage their own neighbourhoods, when social authority is properly incorporated in genuine local institutions, and when there is a clear personal reward for pro-social behaviour, then the deficits we worry about – ignorance and idleness and the rest, including the one Beveridge didn't mention: crime – will decline, and the universal antidote, civilisation, will flourish.

# Manifesto for the tail

**Educational standards**

1. National standards should be strategic and aspirational, setting an overall framework towards which the nation, schools and teachers can aspire.

2. Within the existing framework (and not making any assumptions about the replacement of GCSEs by the English Baccalaureate) the principal national objectives should be that:
   - At least 90% of pupils should achieve the standard of five 'good' GCSEs at age 16 by 2020
   - All 11-year-olds (excluding statemented SEN pupils) should achieve at least level 4 in English and maths by the end of primary school by 2017.

3. School floor standards should reflect the national objectives. Primary school floor standards should require a minimum of 80% to achieve level 4 by 2015 and 95% by 2017.

4. Secondary school floor standards should require a minimum of 60% of school pupils to achieve five good GCSEs by 2015 and 90% by 2020.

## OFSTED framework

5. Operating within the national framework of absolute standards, OFSTED criteria for individual school assessment would be based predominantly on progress of all pupils within each year group relative to their prior attainment.

6. The OFSTED inspection framework should ensure that schools are held accountable for the results of all pupils and not just headline or borderline groups.

7. The recent changes to the inspection framework, encompassing low-, middle- and high-attaining groups, improve the focus on the tail. But they should go further and include an explicit focus on schools' success at improving the progress of low attainers and at moving children off the SEN register by targeted catch-up.

## Foundation Years

8. A new set of Life Chances Indicators, monitored and published by the DfE, should be established to run alongside financial measures of poverty.

9. The 'Foundation Years' should be established as a new pillar in the education system with specific national accountability, bringing together all under-5s services, including post-natal classes, the Healthy Child Programme, Sure Start Children's Centres, early years' education and pre-school places. Lessons learned from Sure Start and other efforts to integrate services for children should be taken into account.

## Primary/pupil premium

10. New accountability mechanisms should be introduced for the pupil premium to make funding partly dependent on results, with up to one year of pupil premium allocation contingent on that child attaining basic level 4 literacy at Key Stage 2. The sum would be recoupable if the literacy target is not met, and passed directly to the relevant secondary school, which must use the sum to fund participation for the relevant child in an approved remedial literacy programme.

## Dedicated secondary provision

11. Dedicated secondary provision to be created for low (sub-level 4) attainers at Key Stage 2. Low attainers to be issued with vouchers which enable them to 'purchase' dedicated provision either at state or non-state schools. Providers of dedicated provision to be incentivised through a payment-by-results system.

## Special Educational Needs

12. The SEN designation should be limited to children with a diagnosable learning difficulty and a new category introduced of Additional Educational Needs (AEN) to identify children who need some kind of extra support or intervention, but who do not have any identifiable learning disability.

13. Schools should be acknowledged in OFSTED judgements for using SEN and AEN designation sparingly, especially those with disadvantaged intakes.

14. Individual schools should be expected to have a clear diagnosis of every child designated as having SEN, with a specific individualised learning plan.

**Teachers**

15. Establish a Teacher Priority Programme to attract teachers to disadvantaged schools, with salary supplements for those teachers willing to teach at schools with above twice the average proportion of pupils on free school meals. The supplement would rise to reflect teacher longevity in the new post. Teachers on the programme would be entitled to a Professional Development Guarantee, in the form of a voucher to be redeemed against professional development opportunities.

16. Establish new Teacher Partnership Groups which would deploy teachers into designated Teacher Priority Areas (groups of schools in areas of severe social and economic disadvantage) and enable highly skilled teachers to be deployed across four or five secondary schools.

17. Expand Teach First from the current 1,000 graduates per annum to 5,000 per annum, so that it is supplying one in four new secondary school teachers and as much as half the new teachers for more challenging schools.

18. Expand the existing Teaching Leaders programme, which trains middle leaders for challenging schools, from the current 300 annual graduates to 1,500 annual graduates.


**Curriculum/qualifications for 14- to 16-year-olds**

19. Ensure all children are taught a predominantly academic curriculum to age 16.

20. Introduce qualifications which certify meaningful academic achievement below grade C at GCSE, whether through English Baccalaureate Certificate or otherwise.

### Child and Adolescent Mental Health Services (CAMHS)

21. CAMHS should be integrated closely with local schools, and held accountable for progress of children under their treatment programme (accountability measures should include school attainment and attendance).

22. Attendance rates at CAMHS should be published, including aggregated data on children from poor families and other vulnerable groups.

23. Providers of mental health services who fail across a range of accountability measures should be expected to improve or go out of business.

24. More mental health professionals should be situated in schools so that children and families receive a more 'joined-up' approach to support, moving beyond simple reliance on diagnosis and medication.

### Neighbourhoods

25. Establish new Civil Zones in neighbourhoods of high disadvantage, modelled on Harlem Children's Zone, with multiple interventions, both in-school and out-of-school, to build community and raise children's aspirations and attainment.

### Regions

26. Launch Regional Challenges (modelled on London Challenge, Black Country Challenge and Greater Manchester Challenge) for the worst-performing regions, including designated coastal regions and other poorly performing regions such as Yorkshire,

Humberside and the North East. The Regional Challenge initiatives would specifically target underperforming schools and would encourage the sharing of best practice, collaboration between 'families' of similar schools, targeted interventions for low-attaining pupils.

# Notes

## Chapter 1

1 Absolute Return for Kids, a children's charity.
2 Nationally 18% of children are on Free School Meals.
3 DfE (2010) *Youth Cohort Study and Longitudinal Study of Young People in England: The Activities and Experiences of 18 year olds: England 2009*; OECD (2011), *Education at a Glance*, p. 3910. (2009 study based on 2005/6 GCSE cohort).
4 Civitas (2010) 'Factsheet – Education in Prisons'.
5 DfE Statistical Release: 10–17 year olds brought before the courts for offences relating to the public disorder between 6th and 9th August 2011: background characteristics, school attendance and educational attainment, Oct. 2011.
6 OECD (2011) *Education at a Glance*, p. 39.
7 Defined as a minimum of five grade 1 CSE passes or their O Level equivalent (five grades at A*–C).
8 In 2011, 42% of employers were not satisfied with young people's basic literacy/use of English (only 6% were 'very satisfied'). Nearly two-thirds (65%) of employers saw a 'pressing need to raise standards to literacy and numeracy amongst 14–19 year olds' (CBI Education and Skills survey 2011).
9 OECD (2011) *Strong Performers and Successful Reformers in Education: Lessons from PISA for the United States*, p. 14.
10 'Education at a Glance': OECD Indicators 2012.
11 Claudia Goldin and Lawrence Katz (2010) *The Race Between Education and Technology*, Belknap Press.

12 McKinsey, *The Economic Impact of the Achievement Gap in America's Schools*, April 2009.

13 *The Mobility Manifesto*, Sutton Trust/Boston Consulting Group, March 2010. The calculations are based on the increased lifetime earnings of students as they gain higher levels of qualifications.

14 Italics added.

15 'Because of the pressures we have from the senior management team, we have to give our weaker teachers the lower sets ... because of the pressure of getting the middle kids up to Cs you have to put your most experienced teachers with them' (teacher quoted in 2007 DCSF study).

16 Machin and Vernoit (2011), cited in Chapter 7 of this volume (see page 106).

17 Andrew Adonis (2012) *Education, Education, Education*, Biteback Publishing.

18 Machin and Silva, Chapter 7 of this volume.

19 See Leon Feinstein, *Inequality in the Early Cognitive Development of British Children* (2000), and *Recent Changes in Intergenerational Mobility in the UK*, Sutton Trust (2007).

20 See Chapter 6 of this volume.

21 Waldfogel and Washbrook (2012) *Social Mobility and Education Gaps in the Four Major Anglophone Countries*, Sutton Trust/Carnegie Corporation.

22 See Bassett, Chapter 12 of this volume.

23 Adonis (see note 17).

24 *Aspiration and Attainment amongst Young People in Deprived Communities*, Cabinet Office (2008).

25 Within level 4, there are three sub-grades: level 4c, 4b, 4a.

26 Only 82% of pupils attained level 4 in English, and only 80% in maths.

27 Explored further in Chapter 3 of this volume.

28 Neighbourhood poverty (as measured by Idaci scores), FSM, gender and ethnicity.

29 Leunig and Wyness, Chapter 3 of this volume.

30 Aided by the London Challenge, introduced in 2003.

31 *Raising Young People's Higher Education Aspirations: Teacher Attitudes*, DIUS (2009).

32  That is, 82 percentage points average variation compared with just 22 percentage points. Source: *Education at a Glance*, OECD.

33  *Improving the Impact of Teachers on Pupil Achievement in the UK*, Sutton Trust, September 2011.

34  Defined as a teacher in the 16th percentile according to value added scores.

35  Defined as 84th percentile according to value added scores.

36  *Students with Disabilities, Learning Difficulties and Disadvantages*, OECD (2007).

37  OECD (see note 9).

## Chapter 2

1  DfE press release: http://www.education.gov.uk/inthenews/inthenews/a0070042/major-international-study-shows-englands-15-year-olds-performing-poorly-in-mathematics-science-and-reading

2  Centre for Social Justice (2007) *Breakthrough Britain: Educational Failure*.

3  OECD (2010) *PISA 2009 Results: Overcoming Social Background – Equity in Learning Opportunities and Outcomes* (Volume II).

4  Gebhardt, E. and Adams, R. (2007) 'The Influence of Equating Methodology on Reported Trends in PISA', *Journal of Applied Measurement*, 8, 3, 305–322.

5  Braconier, H. (2012) *Reforming Education in England*, OECD Economics Department Working Paper No. 939, OECD Publishing.

6  Machin, S. and Vignoles, A. (2005) *What's the Good of Education? The Economics of Education in the UK*, Princeton, Princeton University Press.

7  McIntosh, S. (2004) *The Impact of Vocational Qualifications on the Labour Market Outcomes of Low-Achieving School-Leavers*, CEP discussion paper 621.

8  De Coulon, A., Marcenaro-Guitierrez, O., Vignoles, A. (2008) *The Value of Basic Skills in the British Labour Market*, EEDP, 77. Centre for the Economics of Education, London School of Economics and Political Science.

9   Machin and Vignoles (see note 6), p. 224.

10  Ashworth, J. (1988) 'A Waste of Resource? Social Rates of Return
    to Higher Education in the 1990s', *Education Economics*, 6, 27–44;
    Murphy, J. (1993) 'A Degree of Waste', *Oxford Review of Education*,
    20, 81–82; Robinson, P. (1997) *Measure for Measure: a Critical Note
    on the National Targets for Education and Training and International
    Comparisons of Educational Attainment*, LSE discussion paper 355.

11  Includes variation both between schools and within schools that could
    be explained by economic, social and cultural status as measured by the
    associated PISA index.

12  In the PISA study an index was compiled that describes relative
    economic, social and cultural status of the participants. It does so
    by combining proxy measures of the student's familial occupation,
    education and possessions. The highest occupational status and
    education level of the father or mother are used. The survey enquired
    about possession of household items indicative of wealth: for example,
    access to the internet, having books of poetry at home, or a desk to work
    at.

13  John Jerrim, 'The Socio-Economic Gradient in Teenagers' Reading
    Skills: How Does England Compare with Other Countries?', Institute
    for Fiscal Studies, *Fiscal Studies*, 33, 2, 159–184.

14  Germany provides an extreme contrast: at the low end of the
    achievement range outcomes are very strongly associated with family
    background, but at the high end the association is far weaker.

15  National Pupil Database (2011).

16  Layard, R. and Dunn, J. (2009) *A Good Childhood: Searching for
    Values in a Competitive Age*, London, Penguin.

17  Balfour, A., Morgan, M. and Vincent, C. (2012) *How Couple
    Relationships Shape Our World: Clinical Practice, Research and Policy
    Perspectives*, Great Britain, Karnac Books.

18  Harold, G., Aitken, J. and Shelton, K. (2007) 'Inter-Parental Conflict
    and Children's Academic Attainment: a Longitudinal Analysis', *Journal
    of Child Psychology and Psychiatry*, 48, 12.

19  The poorest 13.6% of super output areas, to correspond approximately
    with the 13.6% of the GCSE cohort that is eligible for free school
    meals.

20  Lupton, R. (2006) 'How Does Place Affect Education', in Delorenzi,
    S. (ed.), *Going Places: Neighbourhood, Ethnicity and Social Mobility*,
    London, Institute of Public Policy Research.
21  Thrupp, M., Lauder, H. and Robinson, T. (2002) 'School Composition
    and Peer Effects', *International Journal of Educational Research*, 37,
    5, pp. 483–504; Nash, R. (2003) 'Is the School Composition Effect
    Real?: A Discussion with Evidence from the UK PISA Data', *School
    Effectiveness and School Improvement: An International Journal of
    Research, Policy and Practice*, 14, 4.
22  Leckie, G. (2009) 'The Complexity of School and Neighbourhood
    Effects and Movements of Pupils on School Differences in Models of
    Educational Achievement', *Journal of the Royal Statistical Society*,
    Series A (172), 537–554; Sammons, P., Sylva, K., Melhuish, E.,
    Siraj-Blatchford, I., Taggart, B., Toth, K., Draghici, D. and Smees, R.
    (2011) *Influences on Students' Attainment and Progress in Key Stage
    3: Academic Outcomes in English, Mathematics and Science in Year 9*,
    Institute of Education, University of London.

## Chapter 3

1   In all cases our figures refer to those in state schools.
2   All numbers from the Labour Force Survey, 2011.
3   We also ran the same analysis looking at the top five GCSEs in any
    subject, the top eight including English and maths, and the top eight
    in any subject, as well as at each of these categories excluding non-
    GCSE equivalent qualifications. The measure picked makes very little
    difference to the results.
4   More formally, we regress performance on characteristics and local
    authorities, with Tower Hamlets as the omitted category.
5   There would also be a reduction of 1,000 within London, were laggard
    London boroughs to reach the London average.
6   In this case a further 6,000 London children would also move out of the
    tail.
7   In some cases, of course, an individual not in work has a partner in
    work. Nevertheless, assortative matching in the marriage market means

that the well educated are most likely to pair with the most educated, and the least educated with the least educated.

## Chapter 5

1   Field, F. (2010) *The Foundation Years: Preventing Poor Children Becoming Poor Adults*, London, HM Government.

2   Feinstein, L. (2003) 'Inequality in the Early Cognitive Development of Children in the Early 1970 Cohort', *Economica*, vol. 70, 277, pp. 73–97.

3   Blanden, J. and Gregg, P. (2004) *Family Income and Educational Attainment: A Review of Approaches and Evidence for Britain*, CMPO Working Paper Series, No. 04/101, Bristol University.

4   Office for National Statistics, *GCSE and Equivalent Attainment by Pupil Characteristics in England, 2010/11*, SFR 03/2012, Department for Education, 9 February 2012.

5   Only the performance gap for the British Gypsy/Roma ethnic group is smaller than that for the British Chinese ethnic group, and this is due only to the very low attainment levels of all British Gypsy/Roma children.

6   The three best-performing socio-economic/ethnic groups are: poorer Chinese (73%); richer Indian (76%); and richer Chinese (80%), all measured on five GCSE passes at grades A*–C including English and mathematics.

7   Feinstein, L. (2003) *How Early Can We Predict Future Education Achievement?* CentrePiece, London School of Economics.

8   Gregg, P. and Goodman, A. (2010) *Children's Educational Outcomes: The Role of Attitudes and Behaviours, from Early Childhood to Late Adolescence*, CMPO, University of Bristol and Institute for Fiscal Studies.

9   Ibid.

10  Ibid.

11  A good level of development is commonly accepted to mean good levels of personal, social and emotional development, and good communication, language and literacy skills.

12 Office for National Statistics, *Early Years Foundation Stage Profile Results in England, 2011/12*. SFR 23/2012, Department for Education, 17 October 2012.

13 Sylva, K., Melhuish, E., Sammons, P., Siraj-Blatchford, I., and Taggart, B. (2004) *The Effective Provision of Pre-school Education (EPPE) Project: Final Report. Findings from Pre-school to the End of Key Stage 1*, London, Department for Education and Skills.

14 Perry, B. (2002) 'Childhood Experience and the Expression of Genetic Potential: What Childhood Neglect Tells us about Nature and Nurture', *Brain and Mind*, 3, 1, 79–100.

15 Gregg and Goodman (see note 8).

16 Sylva et al. (see note 13).

17 Gregg and Goodman (see note 8).

18 Waldfogel, J. and Washbrook, E. (2009) 'Income-Related Gaps in School Readiness in the US and UK', APPAM Fall Research Conference.

19 Asmussen, K. and Weizel, K. (2010) *Evaluating the Evidence: Fathers, Families and Children*, King's College London, National Academy of Parenting Research, London.

20 Waylen, A. and Stewart-Brown, S. (2010) 'Factors Influencing Parenting in Early Childhood: A Prospective Longitudinal Study Focussing on Change', *Child Care Health and Development*, 36, 2, 198–207.

21 Sammons, P. et al. (2004) *EPPE: Tech Paper 8a/b*. 'Measuring the Impact of Pre-School on Children's Cognitive Progress over the Pre-School Period', London, Institute for Education.

22 Sylva et al. (see note 13).

23 Sylva, K., Melhuish, E., Sammons, P., Siraj-Blatchford, I., and Taggart, B. (2008) *EPPE 3–11: Final Report from the Primary Phase: Pre-school, School and Family Influences on Children's Development During Key Stage 2 (Age 7–11)*, DCSF-RR061, London, Department for Children, Schools and Families.

24 Gregg and Goodman (see note 8).

25 Brooks-Gunn, J. et al. (2010) 'Discussion and conclusions', *Monographs of the Society for Research in Child Development*, 75, 2, 96–113.

26  Chowdry, H. et al. (2009) *Drivers and Barriers to Educational Success – Evidence from the Longitudinal Study of Young People in England*, DCSF-RR102, London, Department for Children, Schools and Families.

27  Gregg and Goodman (see note 8).

28  Ibid.

29  Muijs, D., Chapman, C., Collins, A. and Armstrong, P. (2010) *Maximum Impact Evaluation: The Impact of Teach First Teachers in Schools*, Manchester University, at: http://eprints.soton.ac.uk/300958/

30  Field. F. (2010) *The Foundation Years: Preventing Poor Children from Becoming Poor Adults*, London, HM Government.

31  Ibid., p. 93.

32  Washbrook, E. (2010) *Early Environments and Child Outcomes*, University of Bristol, p. 7.

33  Ibid.

34  Nowak, C. and Heinrichs, N. (2008) 'A Comprehensive Meta-Analysis of Triple P – Positive Parenting Program Using Hierarchical Linear Modelling: Effectiveness and Moderating Variables', *Clinical Child and Family Psychology Review, 11, 3,* 114–144.

35  Sylva et al. (see note 13).

36  *Ofsted Annual Report 2010–11*, November 2011.

37  Smith, R. et al. (2010) *Childcare and Early Years Survey of Parents 2009*, Natcen, DfE Research Report RR_054, London, Department for Children, Schools and Families.

38  Melhuish, E. et al. (2008) 'Effects of Fully-Established Sure Start Local Programmes on 3-Year-Old Children and their Families Living in England: A Quasi-Experimental Observational Study', *The Lancet*, 372, 9650, 1641–1647.

39  Melhuish, E. et al. (2010) *The Impact of Sure Start Local Programmes on Five Year Olds and their Families*, Research Report DFE-RR067, London, Department for Education, p. viii.

40  Ibid.

41  'Tackling Child Poverty and Improving Life Chances: Consulting on a New Approach' (2010), consultation paper, Department for Education.

42  Hansard, Written Answer, 31 March 2011, columns 500–501W.

43  Calculations from PISA.

44 Bramley, G. and Watkins, D. (2008) *The Public Service Cost of Child Poverty*, Joseph Rowntree Foundation, York.


## Chapter 6

1   Nick Clegg, '£10m to Boost Literacy for Year Sevens', 14 May 2012. (www.dpm.cabinetoffice.gov.uk/news/10m-boost-literacy-year-sevens).
2   Rose, J. (2006) *Independent Review of Early Reading*, final report, London, Department for Education and Skills/TSO.
3   KPMG (2009) 'The Long-Term Costs of Literacy Difficulties' (www. kpmg.co.uk/pubs/ECR2006.pdf).
4   Ibid.
5   Ibid.
6   Pritchard, C. and Butler, A. (2000) 'A Follow-Up Study of Criminality [...]', *International Journal of Adolescent Medicine and Health*, 12, 2–3.
7   World Literacy Foundation (2012) *The Economic & Social Cost of Illiteracy*.
8   National Literacy Trust (2012) *Literacy: State of the Nation*.
9   National Literacy Trust (2011) *Literacy: A Route to Addressing Child Poverty?*
10  KPMG (see note 3).
11  Ruben, R.J. (2000) 'Redefining the Survival of the Fittest: Communication Disorders in the 21st Century,' *The Laryngoscope*, 110, 241.
12  World Literacy Foundation (see note 7).
13  KPMG (see note 3).
14  UNESCO and UNICEF (2007) *A Human Rights-Based Approach to Education*, United Nations Children's Fund and United Nations Educational, Scientific and Cultural Organization, New York and Paris.
15  National Literacy Trust (see note 9).
16  DfE website, 'Pupil Premium – What You Need to Know' (www. education.gov.uk/schools/pupilsupport/premium/b0076063/pp).
17  Nick Clegg, 'Delivering Education's Progressive Promise: Using the Pupil Premium to Change Lives', 14 May 2012 (www.dpm.cabinetoffice.gov.uk/news/

delivering-education-s-progressive-promise-using-pupil-premium-change-lives); and Michael Gove, 'Government Announces Pupil Premium to Raise Achievement', 26 July 2010 (www.education.gov.uk/inthenews/inthenews/a0063284/government-announces-pupil-premium-to-raise-achievement).

18  David Laws, 'Why I'm Proud of the Pupil Premium', *The Guardian*, 24 October 2010.

19  Ibid.

20  Sutton Trust (2011), 'Toolkit of Strategies to Improve Learning – Summary for Schools, Spending the Pupil Premium'.

21  Sarah Teather (10 July 2012), in BBC report 'Reading and Writing Catch-up Classes for Poorer Pupils' (www.bbc.co.uk/news/education-18780527).

22  DfE, Statistical First Release, 'National Curriculum Assessments at Key Stage 2 in England', 15 December 2011.

23  DfE (2011), *Evaluation of Every Child a Reader*, Research Report DFE-RR114.

24  Nick Clegg (see note 1).

25  Nick Clegg, in Rajeev Syal, 'Nick Clegg to Propose £10,000 Prize to Boost Schools' Performance', *The Guardian*, 14 May 2012.

26  Rick Muir, IPPR, 'Clegg's Pupil Premium Could Be Wasted', 15 May 2012 (www.libdemvoice.org/the-independent-view-cleggs-pupil-premium-could-be-wasted-28524.htm).

27  Sutton Trust, 'Pupil Premium Money will have Limited Impact on Poorer Pupils', 27 July 2012.

28  OFSTED (2012) 'The Pupil Premium', 120197.

29  Sir Michael Wilshaw, BBC News, 20 September 2012.

30  David Laws (see note 18).

31  KPMG (see note 3).

32  Ibid.

33  Nick Clegg (see note 1).

34  A greater portion is likely to come from pupil premium funds when the child has failed in *both* literacy and maths (because the £500 'catch-up' money would be likely to be split).

35  David Laws (see note 18).

36 This would be in direct contrast to the funding for summer schools (and potentially also the new 'catch-up premium'), where the schools still retain complete discretion as to what the money can be spent on.

37 This could also raise the possibility for a further form of payment by results whereby money no longer required for the 'catch-up premium' could be redistributed to primary schools which successfully reduce their annual literacy failure rates. This would in turn enable implementation of the calls from some to 'front-load' pupil premium spending at an early age (where it can make the biggest difference) without the risk that it will be 'wasted' by inefficient schools.

## Chapter 7

1 Correspondence to be sent to Stephen Machin (s.machin@ucl.ac.uk) or Olmo Silva (o.silva@lse.ac.uk). We would like to thank James Vernoit for help with the data and Dale Bassett for insightful comments.

2 Le Grand (1991, 1993), Machin and Vignoles (2005) and Burgess et al. (2006) present a discussion of the English school choice experience, while Hoxby (2004) gives a detailed analysis of the topic for the USA.

3 The English secondary school market also includes a set of independent (private and fee-paying) schools. Their management body makes autonomous decisions in terms of hiring and firing of staff, the teaching content, structure and length of the school day, and the procedures for pupil selection and admissions.

4 Admission to schools is based on parental preference, but over-subscribed schools prioritise pupils on the basis of various school-specific criteria. For secular schools, priority is given to children with special educational needs, children with siblings in the school and children who live closest. For Faith schools, regular attendance at local designated churches is foremost. More details are provided in Gibbons et al. (2008).

5 Note that some academies were also introduced as new schools in some particular areas, or as a way for successful (mainly private, fee-charging) schools to expand their pupil intake.

6   As of 7 September 2012, the number of open academies had expanded hugely to 2,309.
7   More details on the introduction and functioning of the Labour academies can be found in Machin and Wilson (2008), Machin and Vernoit (2011) and Wilson (2011).
8   More details about our regressions are provided in the note to Table 7.1.
9   Note that there are also a number of studies not based on lotteries. For example, using propensity score matching, CREDO (2009) shows that charter schools are no better (or worse) than neighbouring traditional public schools. However, results from non-experimental methods are prone to biases due to students' selection into schools; see discussion in Hoxby and Murarka (2007).

## Chapter 8

1   I am deliberately avoiding the perennial debate about whether the ability to read and write and understand and use certain mathematical concepts is English or literacy, mathematics or numeracy. There are true believers in each camp and the by-product of the arguments for secondary students has been the development of qualifications such as core, key and functional skills. Since I'm concentrating on curriculum for 14- to 16-year-olds, who for the most part are engaged with the national curriculum, the debate is less relevant – the vast majority of them, including most of the 'tail', take GCSEs in English and mathematics.
2   I am using the term vocationally related, rather than vocational or occupational, because most of these qualifications introduce learners to a general work-related area and do not equip them with employment competence.

## Chapter 9

1   Special Educational Needs Code of Practice, 2001.
2   Pupils with SEN are, according to the government's definition, those 'with learning difficulties or disabilities that make it harder for them

to learn than most pupils of the same age'. *Special Educational Needs Information Act – An Analysis*, Department for Education, April 2011, p. 3.

3  OFSTED (2010) *The Special Educational Needs and Disability Review*.

4  This includes three categories: School Action (approx. 916,000 pupils), School Action Plus (approx. 496,000 pupils) and Statement (approx. 221,000 pupils). Source: House of Commons Library Briefing, September 2012.

5  *Special Educational Needs Information Act – An Analysis*, Department for Education, April 2011.

6  Department for Education response to Freedom of Information request, January 2011.

7  OFSTED (see note 3).

8  Department for Education (see note 5), p. 19.

9  *Support and Aspiration: A New Approach to Special Educational Needs and Disability*, Green Paper, March 2011, p. 67.

10  http://www.education.gov.uk/rsgateway/DB/SFR/s001075/sfr14–2012v2.pdf

11  ARK Schools is an education charity that runs (as of September 2012) 18 academies in London, Birmingham and Portsmouth. These are a mixture of primary, secondary and all-through (age 3–18) academies. They include new-start schools in areas of high need and formerly under-performing schools that have become ARK academies at the request of the DfE.

12  Amongst the five ARK academies with KS4 pupils in 2011, 36% had lower-than-average attainment on entry in Year 7, compared with a national average of 18%. Source: ARK Schools analysis from 2011 DfE performance tables.

13  ARK Schools data and national data.

14  Source: ARK Schools analysis from 2011 DfE performance tables.

15  'We propose to introduce a new single category of SEN to make sure the right support to raise attainment is given to the right children – replace the existing complicated school action and school action plus systems – and we will provide tighter guidance on which children should be identified as having SEN.' DfE press notice, 15 May 2012.

## Chapter 10

1  Cook, C. (2012) 'The Social Mobility Challenge for School Reformers', *Financial Times*, 22 February 2012, at http://blogs.ft.com/ftdata/2012/02/22/social-mobility-and-schools/#axzz1nIj2Jgqe

2  Allen, R. (2012) 'The Social Mobility Challenge is not Impossible', at www.rebeccaallen.co.uk.

3  Barber, M. and Mourshed, M. (2007) *How the World's Best-Performing School Systems Come Out on Top*, London and New York, McKinsey, p. 13.

4  Schwartz, R. (2009) 'Attracting and Retaining Teachers', OECD Observer, at http://www.oecdobserver.org/news/fullstory.php/aid/2235/Attracting_and_retaining_teachers.html

5  Whelan, F. (2009) *Lessons Learned: How Good Policies Produce Better Schools*, London, Fenton Whelan, pp. 33–5.

6  Levin, B. (2008) *How to Change 5000 Schools*, Cambridge, MA, Harvard Education Press.

7  Machin, S. and Murphy, S. (2011) *Improving the Impact of Teachers on Pupil Achievement in the UK – Interim Findings*, London, Sutton Trust, p. 5.

8  Ronfeldt, M., Lankford, H., Loeb, S. and Wykoff, J. (2011) 'How Teacher Turnover Harms Student Achievement', National Bureau of Economic Research, Working Paper 17176, at http://ww.nber.org.papers/w17176

9  Hanushek, E., Sivkin, S. and Kain, J. (2005) 'Teachers, Schools and Academic Achievement', *Econometrica*, 73, 2, 417–458.

10  Allen, R. and Burgess, S. (2012) 'Why the New School League Tables are Much Better ... and Could Be Better Still', at http://cmpo.wordpress.com/2012/01/25/why-the-new-school-league-tables-are-much-better-but-could-be-better-still/

11  I should like to thank my colleague Emma Wisby for her detailed advice on ideas in this chapter.

## Chapter 11

1 Sutton Trust (2011), *Improving the Impact of Teachers on Pupil Achievement in the UK – interim findings*.

2 McKinsey (2009), *Capturing the Leadership Premium*.

3 OECD (2009) *PISA 2009 Results: Overcoming Social Background, Equity in Learning Opportunities and Outcomes*.

4 Financial Times blog (http://blogs.ft.com/ftdata/2012/02/22/social-mobility-and-schools/) (Chris Cook, 22 February 2012).

5 Department for Education, 2011 Performance Tables (http://www.education.gov.uk/schools/performance/).

6 Department for Education, *The Importance of Teaching* (White Paper, 2010).

7 Education Select Committee (2012) *Great Teachers: Attracting, Training and Retaining the Best*.

8 Leunig and Wyness, Chapter 3 of this volume.

9 *NQT Quality Improvement Study for the Training and Development Agency for Schools*, Centre for Education and Inclusion Research and Division of Education and Humanities Sheffield Hallam University, p. 11.

10 OECD (see note 3).

11 Sutton Trust (see note 1).

12 Department for Education (see note 6).

13 Education Select Committee (see note 7).

14 Education Select Committee (see note 7).

15 Eligibility criteria for Teach First (50% of children in bottom 30% of IDACI measure), Teaching Leaders and Future Leaders (IDACI measure, greater than 15% of children receiving Free-School Meals, school's five A*–C achievement less than 40%).

16 Teach First Annual Review 2011.

17 Schleicher (2012) 'Value for Money in Schools', Reform conference.

## Chapter 12

1   The author is writing in a personal capacity; the views expressed do not represent those of his employer. Many thanks to Olmo Silva and Will Tanner for reviewing drafts, and to Rob Greig for assisting with research.
2   Thanks to Chris Cook for his analysis.
3   It should be noted that direct causation between the Opportunity Scholarship Programme and improvements in outcomes cannot be identified, since other educational reforms were taking place simultaneously. However, the evaluative studies referenced here are methodologically valid, comparing outcomes of participating pupils (chosen at random) with those of a control group of pupils who were eligible and wished to participate in the programme but were unable to do so due to capacity constraints.

## Chapter 13

1   Grant Smith, Brad Jongeling, Petra Hartmann, Craig Russell and Lou Landau (2010) *Raine ADHD Study: Long-term outcomes associated with stimulant medication in the treatment of ADHD in children*, Government of Western Australia, Department of Health.

## Chapter 14

1   John Bowlby (1969) *Attachment*, Basic Books.
2   See Chapters 1 and 2 of this volume.
3   Granovetter (1973) 'The Strength of Weak Ties', *American Journal of Sociology*, 78, 6, 1360–1380.
4   'Joint enterprise', the legal doctrine that one can bear responsibility for the actions of one's comrades (e.g. a fellow gang member), is a controversial, and perhaps flawed, attempt to bring 'relationism' into criminal justice.

5  Wikström et al. (2012) *Breaking Rules: The Social and Situational Dynamics of Young People's Urban Crime*, Clarendon Press.

6  Hernando de Soto (1985) *The Other Path: The Invisible Revolution in the Third World*, HarperCollins.

7  Maruna and LeBel (2003) 'Welcome Home? Examining the "Re-Entry Court" Concept from a Strengths-Based Perspective', *Western Criminology Review*, 4 2, 91–107.

8  Jonathan Sachs (2000) *The Politics of Hope*, Vintage.

9  This argument was well made by Oliver Letwin in the 2003 Keith Joseph Memorial Lecture: 'What is the opposite of crime? Some would say "order", but that is no more than the absence of crime while what we seek is something that is in active opposition to it. Crime is a destructive force; its opposite must be a constructive force. In modern English idiom, this constructive force goes unnamed. It is a symptom, and perhaps to a slight degree a cause, of the failure of our society to overcome crime that we have no word for its opposite. This is not true of all languages and cultures. There is, for example, the Hebrew word shalom. The inadequate English translation is "peace", but shalom signifies much more than the absence of conflict. The true meaning is more akin to "the wholeness of community", the totality of right relationships within communities, between persons and families and social groups, between man and his environment.'

10  Gary LaFree (1999) *Losing Legitimacy: Street Crime and the Decline of Social Institutions in America*, Westview Press.

11  David Deming (2011) 'Better schools, less crime?', *Quarterly Journal of Economics*, 126, 4, 2063–2115.

12  See Ken Robinson, TED talk 2006, and *Out Of Our Minds: Learning to be Creative*, 2011 (http://www.ted.com/talks/ken_robinson_says_schools_kill_creativity.html).

13  John Abbott (2009) *Overschooled and Undereducated: How the Crisis in Education is Jeopardising our Adolescents*, Continuum.

14  Nick Wilkie et al. (2001) *Hunch: A Vision for Youth in Post-Austerity Britain*, London Youth.

15  Alan Dyson et al. (2012) *Developing Children's Zones for England*, Save the Children.